Financial Ratios and Financial Statement Analysis

Financial Ratios and Financial Statement Analysis

Jagadish R. Raiyani
R. B. Bhatasna

New Century Publications
New Delhi, India

NEW CENTURY PUBLICATIONS
4800/24, Bharat Ram Road,
Ansari Road, Daryaganj,
New Delhi – 110 002 (India)

Tel.: 011-2324 7798, 4358 7398, 6539 6605
Fax: 011-4101 7798
E-mail: indiatax@vsnl.com info@newcenturypublications.com
www.newcenturypublications.com

Editorial office:
LG–7, Aakarshan Bhawan,
4754-57/23, Ansari Road, Daryaganj,
New Delhi – 110 002

Tel.: 011-4356 0919

First Published: **2011**

Reprint: **2023**

ISBN: **978-81-7708-267-8**

Published by New Century Publications and printed at Salasar Imaging Systems, New Delhi.

Designs: Patch Creative Unit, New Delhi.

PRINTED IN INDIA

About the Book

The focus of financial analysis is on key figures in the financial statements and the significant relationship that exists between them. The analysis of financial statement is a process of evaluating the relationship between component parts of financial statements to obtain a better understanding of the position and performance of a firm. The first task of the financial analyst is to select the information relevant to the decision under consideration from the total information contained in the financial statements. The second step is to arrange the information in a way to highlight significant relationships. The final step is interpretation and drawing of inferences and conclusions. In brief, financial analysis is the process of selection, relation and evaluation.

Keeping all this in view, the present book is devoted to an in-depth analysis of financial statements and its use for decision-making by various parties interested in them. The focus of the book is on ratio analysis which is the most widely used technique of financial statement analysis.

About the Authors

Jagadish R. Raiyani is presently Assistant Professor of Commerce, Geetanjali College, Saurashtra University, Rajkot, Gujarat. He has published research papers in reputed journals including *Professional Banker* (ICFAI), *Yojana* (Planning Commission) and *Arthsankalan* (Kurukshetra). He has participated in many National and International level conferences. His research interests include accounting and finance, auditing and taxation.

R.B. Bhatasna is presently Associate Professor, Department of Commerce, Smt. M.T. Dhamsania College, Rajkot, Gujarat. His teaching and research interests include accounting and finance and banking. He has participated in many State, National and International level conferences. His research papers have been published in reputed magazines like *Yojana and Arthsankalan.*

Contents

Preface

The financial sector of India, especially banks, is subject to prudential regulations, both in regard to capital and liquidity. As the current global financial crisis has shown, liquidity risks can rise manifold during a crisis and can pose serious downside risks to macroeconomic and financial stability. Reserve Bank of India (RBI) had already put in place steps to mitigate liquidity risks at the very short-end, risks at the systemic level and at the institution level as well.

Large reliance by banks on borrowed funds can exacerbate vulnerability to external shocks. This has been brought out quite strikingly in the recent financial crisis in the global financial markets. Accordingly, in order to encourage greater reliance on stable sources of funding, RBI has imposed prudential limits on banks on their purchased inter-bank liabilities and these limits are linked to their net worth. Furthermore, the incremental credit deposit ratio of banks is also monitored by RBI since this ratio indicates the extent to which banks are funding credit with borrowings from wholesale markets (now known as purchased funds).

Asset liability management guidelines for dealing with overall asset-liability mismatches take into account both on and off-balance sheet items. Finally, guidelines on securitization of standard assets have laid down a detailed policy on provision of liquidity support to Special Purpose Vehicles (SPVs).

In order to further strengthen capital requirements, the credit conversion factors, risk weights and provisioning requirements for specific off-balance sheet items including derivatives have been reviewed. Furthermore, in India, complex structures like synthetic securitisation have not been permitted so far.

The analysis of financial statement is a process of evaluating the relationship between component parts of financial statements to obtain a better understanding of the firm's position and performance. The focus of financial analysis is on key figures in the financial statements and the significant relationship that exists between them. The first task of the financial analyst is to select the information relevant to the decision under consideration from the total information contained in the financial statements. The second step is to arrange the information in a way to highlight significant relationship. The final step is interpretation and drawing of inferences and conclusions. In brief, financial analysis is the process of selection, relation and evaluation.

Keeping all this in view, the present book is devoted to an in-depth analysis of financial statements and its use for decision making by various parties interested in them. The focus of the book is on ratio analysis as the most widely used technique of financial statement analysis. The importance of ratio analysis and its limitations are briefly outlined in this book.

The book is primarily intended for undergraduate, postgraduate students in commerce and management and chartered and cost accountancy. Those doing similar courses in business management or appearing in the restructured civil services and other competitive examinations will find it equally useful. Its usefulness, however, is not confined to academicians alone. It may also be of special interest to the practitioners in the field.

Finally, we would be failing in our duty if we do not acknowledge the deep debt of gratitude that we owe to the various authors whose writings have provided us insights into the intricacies of the subject.

September 2010 **Jagadish R. Raiyani**
Rajkot **R. B. Bhatasna**

1

Ratio as Aid to Management

1.1 Meaning of Ratio Analysis

The Latin word 'ratio' stands for reason, and so also its derivative 'ratiocinari'. Sister words like 'reri' and 'ratus' imply the need to think. In English language, ‘ratiocinate’ means to reason, whereas 'ratio' stands for the relation or the proportion of one thing to another (along with reason or cause). As applied to mathematics, it is the quotient of one quantity divided by another of the same kind, usually expressed as a fraction, say 1/2 (or 1:2). In the context of music, the term ratio refers to the relation between the vibration numbers of two tones which may be vital for harmony and melody (an agreeable musical air or tune, as against noise or other disagreeable sound).

Such a relationship can be *either* fixed *or* variable. A fixed relationship may subsist between two objects (or parts of an object) of a static character. For example, a piece of land owned by a farmer may have a fixed ratio, between its length and width, so long as it is not sub-divided or consolidated with another pace of land. But the analysis of such a relationship is likely to have little relevance, unless it can be shown that a particular ratio between length and width is optimum or ideal for cultivation (use of mechanical devices, manures, irrigation facilities and the like). Furthermore, it has to be seen if the farmer has a choice between two or more pieces of land having different ratios between length and width (and whether such a choice can be exercised in the midst of historical, sociological, legal and other- constraints).

A fixed ratio can be visualized even between two variables. There is the well known Einsteinium doctrine (relativity theory) to suggest that if two trains are moving at exactly the same speed on two parallel tracks, passengers on either side may seem to feel that none of the trains is in motion. A similar fixed relationship has more recently been established between the earth (which is moving round) and certain communication satellites (also in orbit at fixed angles) through which TV network programmes are telecast. The important point is that the proportion of change in one set of variables should always be equal to (commensurate with) the proportion of chance in the other set of variables. In statistical language, this is a state of perfect positive correlation (+1).

Such a state of affairs can be the one actually obtaining in a given set of circumstances, or it may be thought of as an ideal relationship. For example, a slimming centre may be working on the formula that an adult male should weigh just as many kilograms as the number of inches measuring his height. Thus a 6-ft-tall person weighing 90 kilograms may be called upon to reduce his obesity to a level of 72 (indicating a 20 percent cut in weight to match his height running into 72 inches). Likewise, many public enterprises in India thought it fit to assume 1:1 an ideal equity-debt ratio, so that, out of every governmental allocation of two rupees, one rupee was treated as equity, and the other rupee was put in the category of (interest-bearing and repayable) debt.

A variable relationship is bound to exist between two objects if one of these is of static dimensions, whereas the other one is of a changing character. For example, if a tree is growing by the side of a house whose height is constant, the tree: house (height) ratio may continue to vary, say from 1:2 to 1:1, and thereafter to 2:1. The ratio between two variables, too, would vary if the relative change is not always matching, either because of the varying impact of uncertainty, or due to the fact that one of the variables is inherently subject to a higher magnitude of change (upward or downward). It may also be that considerations of idea! Viability suggests a higher (or lower) proportion of change in one of the variables than in the other. Steel girders used to bridge the span(s) of a river may offer a case in point, if (say) a 20 percent increase in length calls for a 30 percent excavation in width. Likewise (but in a converse direction), the ideal inventory: turnover ratio may vary from 1:3 to 1:4 as the sales volume gets doubled. Thus, as the turnover moves up from Rs. 30,000 to Rs. 60,000, the ideal level of inventory rises from Rs. 10,000 to Rs. 15,000 only and not to Rs. 20,000).

Sometimes the variable relationship between two sets of variables is of an inverse character. As such, art increase in one variable is associated with a decrease in the other. When the rate of increase (in one) is fully matched by the rate of decrease (in the other), it is a state of perfect negative correlation (–1). For example, if the price elasticity of the demand of a commodity is *unity*, this type of relationship subsists between the unit price and the number of units demanded. Thus, when the price per unit is doubled, from Rs. 50 to Rs. 100, the number of units demanded would be reducing to one-half, say from 100 to 50. As such, the total expenditure on the consumption of that commodity would remain constant at Rs 50. Likewise, if a public authority rules that ever agricultural farm-in a particular district would conform to an ideal area (say 6,400 square metres), the relationship between length and width would be inverse (presuming that an individual furrier has some latitude to vary the length and the width, so long as the total area does not depart from the norm).

Thus, if farm is 128 metres long, it will be 50 metres wide; and, if farm B is 100metres long, it will be 64 metres wide. As such, the ratio (A/B) between the lengths of the two farms (128/100) is a reciprocal of the ratio between the widths (50/64) of these farms. However, if a third farm C has dimensions of 80 metres x 80 metres, the practical distinction between length and width disappears (although, in an academic sense, the reciprocal character of the two ratios is still maintained).

This inverse character of relationship may also be

applicable to some of the variables emerging from the Trading/ Profit and Loss Account (Income Statement) and the "Balance Sheet of a business entity. For example, if the payout ratio (proportion of earnings/profits .used for payment of dividend) is high, the retained earnings ratio would be low (and *vice versa*). This stipulation, of course, assumes that 'dividend payment' and 'retention' are the only two outlets for earnings/profits (with the structure of taxation being neutral towards both these outlets). Likewise, the Equity: Total Investment Ratio and Debt: Total Investment Ratio would have an inverse relationship. Assuming that the total investment remains constant between the two consecutive dates of a firm; Balance Sheet, and that equity and debt are the only two sources of investment; a reciprocal relationship would be found to subsist between these two variables. This may be subject to the legal constraint that equity capital, as distinguished from debt, cannot (usually) be paid back to the shareholders of a going concern (though redeemable preference shares may sometimes be deemed to form part of equity, whereas the debt, on the other and, may be of a perpetual character).

In fine, ratio analysis may be defined to mean "the establishment of a reasoned relationship" of a fixed or variable character between measurements of certain phenomena having some kind of linkage. Very often, though not correctly, ratio analysis is dubbed merely as a financial or accounting exercise. It is true that liquidity, solvency, profitability and market test ratios are quite widely used measures. Yet, ratio analysis is not confined to the four walls of financial management. There are vast and fruitful opportunities for its application to production, marketing, personnel, and general management. With regard to production (operations) management, statistical quality control (based on spoilage and other ratios) is a casein point. Further, for a multi-product (say automobile) unit, the ratio(s) in which scooters, cars, vans, jeeps, buses and trucks are to be manufactured may be a most vital one. Such an exercise in product-mix may be based on linear programming or any other modern technique. Likewise, in the domain of marketing management, ratios in the form of reasoned relationships may have to be established between credit and cash sales, between free samples and sales potential, between marketing expenses and sales/revenue, between the cost and benefit of market research/advertising/sales force/after-sales service and all that.

Similarly, in the context of personnel management, it may be vital to keep a close watch on labour turnover ratio, absenteeism ratio, lost mandays ratio and labour productivity ratio, along with other ratios relevant to manpower planning, human resource accounting training, merit rating and the like. So far as general management is concerned, it may (besides making use of vital ratios germane to various functional areas of management) focus attention on reasoned relationships in a broader context, such as social cost-benefit ratio, concentration/diversification ratios and techno-managerial change ratio, besides image building, model building and other sinews of modern management.

1.2 Significance and Limitations of Quantitative Approach to Management

The quantitative approach to management may be said to have manifested itself mainly in three forms. *First*, the theory of probability and other branches of statistics (along with their phenomenal growth) have come in for a great deal of reliance in the decision-making process of modern managers. *Secondly*, and more recently, have come to the fore a variety of quantitative techniques under the umbrella of operational/operations research. *Thirdly,* there are the other applications of mathematics to economics, psychology, sociology and other behavioural studies having their bearing on commercial viability or managerial efficacy of various types of entities. Various factors have added to the significance of quantitative approach in management/administration.

Firstly, it is the tremendous increase in the quantum of activity. In ancient India (roughly synchronizing with the dawn of Christian era in the West), when the volume of business (both domestic trade and foreign commerce) was relatively small, it was quite possible to have 100 percent quality control of goods. Kautilya's *Arthashastra* testifies that this situation actually obtained at that time, when this celebrated writer-economist was operating as administrator-politician under a different name (Chanakya). But, after the appearance of Industrial Revolution (or, rather a series of industrial revolutions, as Professor W.W. Rostow has chosen to-suggest), even conscientious producers and public officials have to rest content with sample checking. In a sense, it is ironical that even quality control has to fall back on quantitative techniques like the theory of probability. As such, it is called 'statistical quality control'. Not only that, where the ratio of substandard items to total output tends to be very low, producers may feel tempted even to give up the quality control drive as such. For example, the (accidentally) unfortunate consumer of a shaving blade, which scratches his skin, may easily be left to his lot (instead of the manufacturer searching for one defective piece in a whole batch of production).

Secondly, technological and other changes have added many new dimensions to managerial decision-making, so that recourse to quantitative approach is vital for identifying important elements of various problems and considering the same in a systematic fashion. Sometimes the use of a computer or computerized man (robot) may appear indispensable in the context of too many complexities, the demand for speedy exercise, and the need for stubbornness in a mission. There may also be the need to re-check the results and re-adjust the strategy from time to time in view of the rapidly changing situation.

Thirdly, where choice has to be made from amongst a large number of (apparently viable) alternatives, quantitative techniques provide the much needed fineness in the process of comparison from time to time on a consistent basis. A standard model may be of considerable utility in this regard. In fact, relativity is the basis not only of modern science but also of contemporary culture and civilization. There is a management joke typifying a situation in which A asks his friend B "how is your wife?" and gets back a retort "as compared to what'?" That is, B's wife may be feeling (today) better in relation to yesterday but worse in relation to the day before yesterday. Alternatively, in a hospital situation, B's wife may be progressing but not as fast as/A's wife. Likewise, the one-eyed may be a privileged lot in an assembly abounding with blind persons, but not so in the midst of those endowed with two eyes each. Applying this to a business situation, the profitability ratio of a firm for a certain year may be compared with its own action in earlier years or with similar ratios of other firms for the same year.

Fourthly, the memory of a computer and other capsule forms be of significant value where managerial problems are of a continuous or repetitive character. The lessons learnt from time to time can be built into a basic model which is able to guide the decision-making process, for a fairly long period. For example, in a social situation, a model can be constructed for matrimonial match-making. This may rest on a number of ratios or reasoned relationships between the attributes of the prospective bride and her groom. These variables may include age, height, weight and the like. As applied to a business entity, one may like to build up a weighted aggregate of ratios (master ratio) as indicator or predictor of industrial sickness, trade cycles and such other situations.

Fifthly, a mathematical model or other quantitative apparatus can be a valuable tool for managerial communication and also for ensuring a critical minimum of uniformity in decision-making. Further, for implementing decisions, the model can be a useful frame of reference. For example, how should a big commercial bank, like the State Bank of India, having thousands of branches within and outside the country, give some kind of objectivity to its discretion in accepting or rejecting loan applications? This can be done through the prescription of ideal (minimum/ maximum) norms as typified by profitability, liquidity and solvency ratios or other quantitative indicators seeking to distinguish sick units from the healthy lot. The computerization of Indian Airlines bookings (March 1985) was designed, inter alia, to allay suspicion regarding the abuse of human discretion and to build up an image of objectivity.

Finally, the quantitative approach has assumed overriding significance, almost in every quarter, because the language of numbers seems to carry much greater conviction than a description in general terms. When the Chairman tells the shareholders that their Company has done extremely well, the statement is not likely to be taken seriously; in any case, it may create widely varying vibrations amongst cross-section of the audience. As against this, a statement to the effect that the ratio of profits/dividends to investment equity has, gone up from 15 percent to 20 percent would instantly be interpreted as a plus point by the bulk of shareholders, even if some of them feel that the management could have performed still better.

The same thing would apply to a Minister (or other official spokesman) trying to convince Parliament (or other assembly of people's representatives) regarding the success of development plans, financial discipline, control of inflation and the like. In fact, any mistake in statistics placed before Parliament may at once attract the "privilege" issue, whereas such an eventuality is unlikely when only general and vague statements are made. For example, when Mr. M. Hidayatullah was the Vice-President of India (1979-84), and ex-officio Chairman of the Rajya Sabha (upper house of Parliament), a member requested him to explain the difference between two replies which the Minister concerned had given on the same question with a certain time gap. The Chairman, with his outstanding legal writ, ruled: "When the Government says that 'the matter is receiving attention' it means that even the file has not been traced; a later statement to the effect that 'the matter is under active consideration' implies that the Government have succeeded in tracing the file."

The above-mentioned example is some kind of a pointer toward the limitations of quantitative approach and, there are many.

Firstly, almost every mathematical or analytical model rests on a set of assumptions which do not necessarily depict the real life situation. Thus, even when a quantitative technique is straight and unambiguous, leading to one precise result only, the conclusion may get grossly vitiated, in case there is a small snag in any assumption, or if certain imponderables have been left out of account. Moreover, a manager or (even) a specialist may not have adequate time, aptitude or (even) expertise to verify the accuracy of his own mathematical exercise, whereas anybody else may suffer from personal delicacy, ignorance and other limitations in checking or reviewing the work of a colleague. Thus, miscalculations even in the mathematical part cannot be ruled out. And a small deviation at an early stage (as with the path of a spaceship destined to reach a particular planet) may ultimately mean missing the target by a wide margin; maybe, one in search of excellence is led seriously astray.

Secondly, the quantitative approach may be abused as an excuse for not exercising common sense, for shirking responsibility, or even for resorting to irresponsible decision-making on the part of managers. For example, a borrowing firm, which has already defaulted several times in the recent past with regard to its interest/repayment obligations (or whose reputation in the market is otherwise quite bad), can succeed in getting another loan at the hands of a bank manager who shuts his eyes to everything else except a few financial ratios which, somehow, may appear close to the normal expectation. Such a manager may not be less dangerous than a physician who blindly relies on the reports of pathological tests, and who simply ignores the suffering of the patient (as narrated by him or as revealed from his demeanour). That, in a way, is the darker side of sophisticated science and technology leading to the appearance of a peculiar inertia. The result is that the modern physician is rarely, if ever, prepared to exert himself in writing out a specific prescription of mixture even for abnormal ailments; for, the recourse to patient compound is so handy and also convenient from the standpoint of evading personal responsibility for the possible adverse reactions of the treatment decided upon. To alleviate this situation, there has been a revival of the general physician's course for overseeing the blind alleys of specialists. No wonder, the business world, too, needs "commonsense management" to supplement the quantitative approach.

Thirdly, there is vast scope for window-dressing in accounting and for the manipulation of financial ratios in particular. This hazard is much greater than what might obtain with regard to medical diagnosis; for, wherever financial parameters are used, there is the inherent problem of valuation. And this difficulty gets accentuated in an era of monetary instability manifesting inflation, recession, stagflation and the like. For example, there can be so many variants of depreciation which may be provided at historical cost, at current cost, at future replacement cost, or not provided at all (when price rise more than compensates, in monetary terms, the gradual diminution in the value of an asset as a result of its use). In fact, even the relationships between current items may not be quite reliable when taxes, costs, prices, valuation criteria and other business/accounting practices are in a state of flux. Moreover, the greater the reliance placed on quantitative indicators, the greater is the motivation to cook up these parameters or even the data emanating from surveys. As such, researches may get afflicted by dangerous bias dictated by the overriding need to get quantitative results of a particular nature (whether through professional consultants or internal research units).

Fourthly, it is not always easy to find out if a particular relationship (ratio, correlation, association of attributes, or the like) is, in essence, fortuitous (accidental) or based on some kind of cause and effect (or other significant linkage). And a managerial decision taken on the basis of phoney quantitative relationships cannot be said to be rational or scientific. For example, the ratio of sales to net assets may be continuously rising over a number of years, because the numerator (sales) is getting artificially inflated, either due to monetary factors or on account of scarcity conditions deliberately created by a few leading firms in the line. As against this, the denominator (net assets) does not normally go up in spite of phenomenal escalation in the current cost of acquiring fixed assets. On the contrary, liberal depreciation policies may have substantially reduced the denominator, thus giving a totally illusory picture of the growth or efficiency of a particular firm. In point of fact, the sales in physical terms, or even the market share of that firm, may have actually declined over the years in respect of the product under reference. It could be the other way also. That is, in certain situations, a ratio or other quantitative indicator may tend to understate the real status of an undertaking.

Finally, the quantitative approach to management tends to eclipse the qualitative dimensions as also individual instances-of an extreme character either way (efficiency or inefficiency). As such, the image of an organization may not rise or fall *pari passu* with the numerical indices of achievement. For example, the efficacy ratio of a drug may be quite high, say 95 percent; yet, its image in the market may be very poor even if 1 percent of the units produced are so substandard as may cause adverse reaction dangerous enough to result in instantaneous death. Likewise, a decline in the number of disputes or in the ratio of mandays lost does not necessarily make for an improvement in the industrial relations situation' or in the productivity outlook.

Such an approach may simply fail to assess the impact of a "go-slow-movement'" or "work-to-rule campaign" which may be operating particularly in giant undertakings of the public sector. Moreover, a single dispute or tragedy in a particular year (like the Union Carbide gas leakage in 1984 at Bhopal) may turn out to be more crucial and damaging for the image of an organization than a long series of disputes or accidents in an earlier period. It may be so because of an attitude adopted by the management which passes as patently unreasonable not only at the hands of the workers involved, but v also in the detached judgment of the people at large and the official custodians of public morality. The fact remains that many crucial decisions, in the ultimate analysis, are intuitive (based on the so-called horse sense or heuristic programming). It is perhaps equally true that the human mind continues to be the best computer; for, in certain respects, it scores over a glittering galaxy of the consecutive generations of mechanical computers/robots.

1.3. Usage of Ratios vis-à-vis Other Techniques

Four principal techniques seem to deserve mention in the domain of financial management. First, of course, is the ratio analysis. Usually 'it is a relationship between two items appearing in the Balance Sheet, or in the Profit and Loss Account (or one item in the Balance Sheet, and another one in the Profit and Loss Account). When both the items relate to the Balance Sheet, the focus is on a particular point of lime (close of business on a specific date). In this category falls (possibly the most widely used) Current Ratio (Current Assets: Current Liabilities). And there is the well known rule of thumb (2:1) suggesting that a line, whose current assets appear at about twice the figure of current liabilities, passes the test of financial soundness. However, the actual business world may call for widely varying norms tuned to time, type of industry, locality, and all that. Where both the variables emerge from the Profit and Loss Account, the focus is on a particular period (the accounting year). This is the case with Operating Ratio (Operating Cost: Operating revenue or cost of goods sold pins operating expenses: sales) used by transport and other service undertakings, to indicate the extent to which their revenue/gross income from operations is consumed by cost/expenses relevant to those operations as such during the accounting period under reference.

Thus, an Operating Ratio standing at 85 percent implies a Profit Margin of 15 percent. In case one of the variables is drawn from the Balance Sheet, and another one from the Profit and Loss Account, it is a mixture of focus on a date and over a period. The Debtors' Ratio (Debtors: Credit Sales.) furnishes an example of such focus. Trade debtors (book debts/accounts receivable) stand in the Balance Sheet at the close of business on the last day of the accounting year, whereas credit sales are spread over the whole year. The Debtors' Ratio points toward the average duration of credit extended to customers (average collection period). It is based on two assumptions:

That the amount of debtors as revealed by the Balance Sheet truly depicts the average level for the year as a whole; and

That the credit sales are uniformly spread out throughout the year (on the basis of standard Terms of credit).

Secondly, there is fund-flow analysis which rests on the Balance Sheet alone, but as on two dates at the end of two consecutive accounting periods respectively. The focus of fund-flow analysis is on change in various items (inflows and outflows) as between two dates. As against this, a ratio just depicts the position of an enterprise at a particular point of time or over a specified duration (without taking any note of change within that period). In some sense, a ratio is comparable to a snapshot taken by a camera at a definite moment. Such a photograph does not give any idea of the tendency, process and direction of change. As against this, the fund-flow statement is something like a running reel (cinema movie) giving an impression of movement "from one state to another.

However, if a series of ratios are worked out for different (consecutive) periods/points of time, ratio analysis may also succeed in giving some impression of continuity or comparability over time. But this would be a study of relative and not absolute change. Fund-flow analysis usually involves the preparation of two statements (although these 'two statements/parts may as well be combined into a single statement dealing with all items appearing in the Balance Sheet). The first part carries the caption 'Statement of Changes in Working Capital, whereas the second one may simply be described as 'Fund-Flow Statement'. The first statement, dealing with changes in current assets and current liabilities, reveals either an increase in working capital or a decrease in working capital. In either case, the balance is carried to the second statement. The second statement contains, besides balance of the first statement, details of changes in all non-current assets and non-current liabilities. The two sides of the second statement (or a combined statement) should always tally like the two sides of a Balance Sheet. However, the two sides of the first statement are not supposed to tally. It may be a sheer chance if they do; and, in that case, only "nil" balance has to be carried from the first statement to the second one. If it is a case of "cash flow" (as distinguished from "fund flow") analysis, non-cash inflows and outflows may get excluded (so that only actual or imputed cash inflows and outflows are taken into account). Here "cash from operations" is the crucial variable.

Thirdly, reference may be made to trend analysis for finding out the direction and extent of change in certain variables, specially, those appearing in the Profit and Loss Account. For example, almost every firm has a special focus on the trend of its sales. The direction may be positive (increasing) or negative (declining), while an almost static (constant) position may manifest itself in certain cases. Sometimes the oscillations may be such as not to establish any definite trend. Or, the short-term behaviour of sales may be different from the long-term trend. In any case, a mere idea regarding the direction of change is not enough. Management may need to know if the sales are:

Increasing at a rising rate,
Increasing at a constant rate,
Increasing at a falling rate,
Decreasing at a falling rate,
Decreasing at a constant rate or
Decreasing at a rising rate.

Incidentally, these six situations are listed in a descending order presuming that growth of sales is the prime requisite for image building. However, in certain cases, the size of sales is deliberately cut to push up prices and promote profitability (the international oil trade over the decade 1973-83 being a case in point). Whatever be the strategy in this regard, the resulting changes from year to year are often measured in terms of percentages calculated either on a fixed base (the initial year of a period being usually treated as the base) or on a shifting base. In either case, percentages are a form of ratios. As such, the trend analysis is quite analogous to ratio analysis; in fact, the former may even appear as a chain ratio system. The index numbers emerging from the trend percentage method may also be put in the form of a chart. The resulting "trend line" may be smooth and straight or rugged and zig-zag. On the same chart, several trend lines may be drawn to represent other variables like net worth, fixed assets, trade creditors and receivables. These lines, when drawn together, provide another dimension of mutual relationship (visual ratios) between various variables over a number of accounting years. The curves can be smoothened by adopting time series/moving averages approach.

Fourthly, one may think of break-even analysis which implies that the management has to "cut" so fine that the total revenue is just equal to total cost (or vice versa, which means just the same). Shakespeare's Merchant of Venice provides an interesting insight into the fineness of such an operation. As ruled by the judge, the moneylender could lake out just the specified quantity of flesh (nothing more and nothing less) out of the borrower's body (provided further, that not a drop of blood falls). This was, obviously, an impossible feat for the moneylender who could get neither the money due nor the impounded "pound of flesh". A precise equation of cost and revenue may be almost as difficult to achieve, particularly in a large, multi-plant and multi-product firm. It is, however, worth noting that break-even analysis takes 1:1 as a target or end-result ratio between total test and total revenue. As such, it is not quite different from ratio analysis. Moreover, break-even .analysis is not confined merely to the location of break-even break even chart). It can be used to arrive at a point-- (sales volume/value) where a specified (targeted) amount of profit (or sometimes loss, as in the case of sales subsidized for the benefit of the poor or other target groups) can be expected.

Thus, break-even analysis, which forms the foundation of profit planning, takes the garb of cost-volume-profit (CVP) analysis in its broader connotation. Most of the calculations in this regard centre round two connected and crucial ratios. The first one is the Variable Cost Ratio. It is a relationship between variable cost and selling price, whether expressed per unit (Variable Cost Per Unit: Selling Price Per Unit), or for the total volume (Total Variable Cost; Total Selling Price or Sales). In either case, the result would be the same since variable costs (by definition) rise or fall in strict proportion to the level of output. And if the selling price per unit is constant at all levels of sales volume, the relationship between variable costs and sales would also be constant all along. The second one (more widely known) is the profit-volume (P/V), marginal income, or contribution ratio. It is arrived at by subtracting the Variable Cost Ratio from one. Thus, one (or 100 if expressed in percentages) is the summation of the two ratios. The P/V Ratio is a valuable key to the solution of complex problems in profit planning, specially, those relating to multi-product firms.

Some other quantitative techniques, not so germane to finance, may be found relevant to other domains of management. First, in this regard, is variance analysis, with probability/sampling and statistical quality control as its functional cousins. The term 'variance' is, however, interpreted quite differently by the accountant and the statistician respectively. To the former, it just implies the difference between actual cost and standard cost. In this context, reference may be made to: Material Price Variance (actual quantity of material multiplied by "standard price minus actual price"); Material Quantity/ Usage Variance (standard price per unit multiplied by "standard quantity minus actual quantity"); Net/Overall Material Variance ("standard price per unit multiplied by standard quantity" minus "actual price per unit multiplied by actual quantity"); Labour Rats Variance (actual hours multiplied by "standard rate minus actual rate"); Labour Time/Efficiency Variance (standard rate multiplied by "standard hours minus actual hours"); Net/Overall Labour Variance ("standard rate multiplied by standard hours" minus "actual rate multiplied by actual hours"); Indirect Cost Efficiency Variance (standard rate multiplied by "standard hours minus actual hours"); and General Efficiency Variance (total standard cost minus total actual cost).

The accountant can think of numerous other terms, such as: Materials Mix Variance and Materials Yield Variance (two components of Materials Usage Variance); Sales Profit/Margin Variance (actual profit minus budgeted profit); Volume Variance, Activity Variance or Capacity Variance (standard fixed overhead cost limits budgeted fixed overhead cost); Idle Time Variance, Controllable Variance, and Calendar Variance (to show how the available working hours as compared with standard working hours affect overhead expenses-maintenance, supervision, idle time expenses, etc.) As a rule positive variance is favourable, while negative variance is unfavourable. Analogous ratios may as well be constructed, say Materials Price Ratio (standard unit cost: actual unit cost) and Labour Usage/Time/Efficiency Ratio (standard hours: actual hours per unit of output). If the resultant figure is more than one, it may pass as positive; a score of one is just average;

and a ratio falling below one would be deemed to be negative.

In the statistician's dictionary, 'The most common measure of central tendency is the *mean*, or *expected* value, denoted by or E (X) where X is the variable and E is the *expectation operator*; and the most common measure of dispersion is the *variance* σ^{2}", whose square root is the standard deviation to σ. The objective may be merely to test if the actual and expected numbers of items in a category differ significantly from each other (*enumeration statistics*). Alternatively, use may be made of the actual variables, specifically to test the differences between.' the means of the categories (*analysis of variance*). This analysis may be "one-way," "two-way" or based on "Latin squares" (analysis of three effects). In the first case (one-way), the objective may be to find out if all the samples come from the same normal population. For example, if may be vital for a steel plant to ensure that iron ore brought from the mines in different wagons/conveyors through railways/ropeways is of sufficiently uniform quality (homogeneous between several samples and within individual samples). The "null hypothesis may be rejected if (after conducting the F-test), the F-Go efficient or Variance Ratio (greater variance/smaller variance—which, in, this case, cannot be less than unity) is found to be too large. In the second case (two-way), the variance exercise is split up into three parts (instead of only the first two parts in one-way analysis of variance) as follows:

Variance between samples as symbolized by vertical, columns;

Variance between samples symbolized by horizontal rows; and

Residual variance.

Here, there are two F-Coefficients or Variance Ratios- (variance between columns/residual variance and variance between rows/residual variance).

In the third case (Latin-square design), the variance exercise is split up into four parts as follows:

columns;
rows;
varieties (treatments); and
residual variance.

In this design (a rectangle divided into a large number of squares), the treatments (varieties of any input) are so allocated/ combined that no treatment (whether read vertically or horizontally) occurs more than once. The results of various (unique) permutations may then be compared minutely. Of course, this males the variance exercise quite complex. Where simplification is aimed at, 'ranking methods may be applied to problems similar to the one-way analysis of variance. Here, readings for all samples are ranked in descending order, and the original values (data) are substituted by ranks for each sample. The-null hypothesis may then be subjected to a Rank Sum Test which is nonparametric (not calling for any assumption regarding the underlying statistical distribution or normality in the-population for the analysis of variance). Obviously, such a test may not be so sensitive, but it may be a useful basis for "concordance" (extent of agreement between judges or members of a selection committee considering/ searching candidates for a particular position or award).

Firstly, probability/sampling and statistical quality control were described above as functional cousins of variance analysis. On account of the variability often inherent in the mass of data used in business, many management problems find their solution via the science of probability and statistics. A big beginning was made in this regard during the seventeenth century when eminent mathematicians came to be invited by their friends who had been ushered into commercial gambling (speculation) as a sequel to the growth of joint stock enterprise and the appearance of commercial revolution. In a pure game of chance, like the unbiased tossing of a normal coin, the probability of getting the head or tail is just one-half (and the larger the number of tosses the nearer might be the actual outcome to this stipulation). The probability of the outcome of events is measured on a scale ranging between zero (0) and one (1), the former indicating that the event is not likely to occur at all, whereas the latter score goes to suggest that its occurrence is absolutely certain. It is on the basis of such score that the Replacement Theory seeks to determine the cut-off point in the life of an equipment (like aircraft) when it must be replaced (or put out of use) for sheer fear of breakdown (the crash of Air-India and Japan Airlines jumbo jets in 1985 having triggered the issue that Boeing 747 should be grounded).

Likewise, many of the samples and tests of significance are based on probabilities. In particular, this is true of random sampling which also known as probability is sampling. It' assumes that every item of the universe (population) has an equal chance of being chosen. The reliability of the results drawn from a sample (as a substitute for census survey) rests on this assumption which is vita] for market research regarding widely used commodities or services. Similarly, acceptance sampling forms an important base for statistical quality control. If the number of defects (or defective units) exceeds a predetermined tolerance limit (or, the actual content of a certain element/property is less than the lower limit or more than the upper limit), the lot is rejected. Process control, which is another basic requirement of statistical quality control, seeks to monitor manufacturing and ensure concurrent evaluation of the properties of items in the "ongoing process'. Control charts can be particularly useful in this regard. If and when the fluctuations and deviations are "out of proportion", corrective-action can be taken before much damage is caused. Moreover, since certain defects can be detected only *within* a process (and not on its completion), vigilance with regard to divergence from standards is vital for guarding against any liability which may emanate from the supply of products which are not "unseaworthy" or "up to the murk".

Secondly (amongst other quantitative techniques), reference may be made to input-output analysis, mainly associated with the name of Wassily W. Leontief, the Leningrad-born professor at Harvard, who won the 1973 Nobel Prize in Economics. However, the credit for an attempt to construct a macro-economic input-output model of the economy can go to Francois Quesnay (a French economist belonging to the group of physiocrats), whose *Tableau Economique*, and its commentary *Maximes*, were both published in 1758. Quesnay's exercise in, social accounting depicted how transactions lowed between three classes:

Landowners;

The farmers and farm-labourers; and

Others ("sterile class").

It was held out that only the agricultural sector produced any surplus value (a proposition carried forward by Karl Marx to suggest that only labour yields surplus value). Professor Leontief success was heralded by a solution of the problem in matrix algebra, followed by the boost given by modern computers to input-output analysis as a practical proposition. The rectangular table (input-output matrix) has rows (indicating how the output of an industry spreads out through the rest of the economy) and columns (revealing the origins of inputs). The table establishes a set of relationship between a given set of demands for limit goods and services, and the implied accounts of manufactured inputs, raw materials and labour required for the same. The elaborate exercise is based on numerous ratios ("input-output" coefficients) revealing the amount of the output of any one group required to produce-one unit of output of each other group, including itself. In its application to micro-economic situations, input-output analysis may verge on factoral productivity (relationship of one input/factor of production with the total output) or, overall productivity) relationship of all the inputs/factors of production with the total output) ratios. Productivity-linked bonus may be provided for individuals groups of workers.

Thirdly, it may be pertinent to dwell briefly on regression analysis (along with correlation and forecasting techniques).

Correlation and regression techniques are in wide use for estimating the relationship between one variable and one or made of other variables. For example, farmers have known intuitively for several thousand years that there is a significant relationship between the amount of rainfall (one of the inputs) and the output of grain (or other agricultural produce). In fact, one of the main crops (comprising, in particular, wheat sown just after the rainy season around October) is known in India as "Rabi" (depending on God, i.e., the amount of rainfall). The" statisticians, economists, and (more recently) econometricians have tried to transform that subjective approach into objective and quantitative parameters. Thus, a coefficient of correlation can be worked out between inches (or centimetres) of rainfall and mounds (or quintals) of produce in a specified area of land. The nature of correlation may be positive or negative where rainfall tends to destroy a particular crop). The sign plus (+) symbolizes positive correlation, whereas the sign minus (-) stands for negative correlation as measured on a numerical scale varying between zero (0) and one (1).

However, these two extreme situations may be rare. It may be more realistic to say that scores varying between zero (0) and 0.2 suggest very weak correction, whereas scores standing between 0.8 and one (1) are indicative of strong correlation. Strong positive correlation implies strong sympathy in both upward and downward movement of two variables, whereas strong negative correlation means strong antipathy in this regards (a sharp fall in one leading to a steep rise in another and vice versa). However, the coefficient of correlation epitomizes only a broad tendency on average and it does not necessarily establish a causal relationship between two variables. For example, if over a period of three decades in India, both the Bank Rate and the expectation of human life doubled, there would be a strong positive correlation between the two, but with hardly any causal relationship.

Even where causality is strong, say between X (money

supply) and Y (price index), it cannot be concluded that money supply is the only factor influencing the price index (notwithstanding the fact that the numerical score of correlation is very high). Exercises given by Milton Friedman and Rose Friedman in their personal statement (Free to Choose, 1980) are cases in point. A regression exercise, too, suffers from the same limitation regarding the finality of causal relationships.

However, it can be used to forecast the dependent variable as a function of one or more of the independent variables. In simple regression there is only one independent variable; it is analogous to simple correlation. If rainfall is treated as an independent variable, and agricultural produce as its dependent variable, regression analysis may be able to estimate the likely level of output if the rainfall were to be of a particular magnitude. Graphic presentation of such an exercise is intended to produce the "best" regression line through a "scatter" of items (or least-squares fit as the "best" obtainable). Various techniques of interpolation (finding the estimated value at a point of time within the given duration) and extrapolation (finding the estimated value at point of time beyond the given duration) are employed for forecasting (say) the population of a locality or country as a basis both for micro-economic decision-making (like the output level of a particular firm) and macro-economic planning (like plan target regarding the output of food grains for the entire nation).

Fourthly, reliance may be placed on network analysis which a generic term covering a number of techniques is used to plan and control projects comprising a set of interrelated events (denoted by circles) and activities (depicted by connecting lines). The idea is to present in a diagram the sequential relationships (the order in which work is to proceed) between the activities/events by a network of lines/circles. The 'technique involves the application of network theory to scheduling problems and is of particular relevance to construction/maintenance industry where prompt/timely completion of projects/repairs is vital on account of financial, military or other strategic considerations. It was extensively used in the United States Navy Special Projects Program Office. The two best known devices under the umbrella of network analysis are Programme Evaluation and Review Technique (PERT) and Critical Path Method (CPM). In 1957, representatives of two large U.S. companies considered the idea of using a network presentation of job relationships instead of the usual bar charts.

When lines for various jobs were drawn, it became feasible to identify the critical job and thus identify a "critical path". This was the advent of CPM. About the same time, in January 1958, a team was commissioned to investigate scheduling problems, research, development and probabilities of meeting planned objectives in connection with the U.S. Polaris Missile Program. Initially, the code name given to the task (PERT) had been narrated as 'Programme Evaluation Research Task'. Later, with the establishment of the system, it was changed to 'Programme Evaluation and Review Technique'. The popularity of this technique was conditioned by the claim that it had saved more than two years on the Polaris Program as an excellent exercise in time management. CPM and PERT network diagrams are similar but the focus of CPM is on activities or operations, whereas PERT is concerned with events (which are the beginning or ending points of various activities/operations). CPM is designed (as a choice amongst alternative routes) to reach the end-point in the shortest time feasible.

It is not necessarily the shortest route, for in certain situations, a longer route is quicker and safer. The choice is made after taking into account the time likely to be consumed in various sequential activities. As a supplement to this, PERT aims at maximum feasible reduction in the time gap between the end of an activity and the beginning of another (the next in sequence) activity (or several activities). Some critical path methods use only one estimate (emanating from conventional studies or an average of several similar tasks) of the time likely to be consumed in an activity. As against this, some of the PERT schemes have been found to call for three estimates which may emerge from the varying judgments of three individuals, or just indicate the range of time deemed proper by a single judge. The lowest estimate (*a*) is called optimistic; the highest one (*b*) is termed pessimistic; and a third one between the two (*m*) is known as the most likely. The expected time may then be determined on the basis of a weighted average.

Finally, the following other bases of quantitative approach to management are being briefly referred to.

1.3.1 Linear Programming (LP): A more generic term in operational research is *mathematical programming* meant to resolve resource allocation problems. However, LP is the most well known member of this family, in spite of the fact that its application is limited to situations where relationships between variables are *linear*. That is, if one chair costs Rs. 100 and its wood content amount to Rs. 20, ten chairs would cost Rs. 1,000 with a wood content of Rs. 200. When presented on graph paper, these cost curves would, in fact, be straight lines. Likewise, cost curves (straight lines) can be drawn for tables and other items of furniture. And through LP the dealer can decide the number of chairs, tables and other items that he should manufacture (product-mix decision) with a view to maximizing profit. Similarly, LP can be used to arrive at certain decisions (say regarding the location of assembly/storage points) for minimizing the cost (of transportation). This is called the transportation method (model) which can be used also to locate military airfields, petrol tanks, etc. for bombardment of enemy installations at lowest cost/with maximum efficacy. Assign method, used to find the best way of assigning workers to jobs, is another sub-technique of LP.

However, the simplex method is most widely used for solving linear programming problems (optimization of a linear objective function subject to certain constraints). The simplex matrix may have a ratio column also, leading to the location of the key row (with the feast positive ratio) and the key figure ((he number at the intersection of key column and key row). When the relationships between variables are non-linear, quadratic programming (if there is a "squared" relationship between certain variables) and stochastic programming (if there is uncertainty regarding the precise relationships between some variables) may be used. In case the relationships are both linear and non-linear, *integer programming* may be resorted to. Dynamic programming is the mathematical technique to be employed for forging an optimal policy (optimal decision rules through all stages) where a series of interrelated (sequential) decisions are required.

1.3.2 Queuing (Waiting Lines) Theory: This is an exercise in time management vital not only for dealing with customers arriving at crowded service stations/booking windows/bank counters, but also for saving the working time of an organization's own employees (say, when issuing raw materials or collecting back processed goods), it is no less important in the domain of public administration for effecting macro-saving in time as also for keeping the people satisfied. For example, in April 1985, the Government of Rajasthan applied this theory (consciously or sub-consciously) to the collection of annual road tax for the year 1985-86 from owners of motor vehicles in Jaipur. As the last date (April 30) drew near, so many cash and other counters were opened for the issue of vehicle tokens that few had to stand in the queue for more than five-minutes at the head office (as against the usual one hour or more). Here, the cost of an additional counter has to be measured against the likely benefit (as measured by saving in time, reduction in overheads, increase in revenue, higher level-of satisfaction on the part of customers/workers/people in general, etc.) In this context, the mathematical exercise seeks to ascertain mainly three things:

The probability of getting delayed;

The average number of people likely to be keep waiting; and

The average wailing time.

During 1986-87, the policy of "one-time collection" (equal to ten years' road tax) was adopted.

1.3.3 Game Theory: Developed by John Von Neumann and Oscar Morgenstern, it seeks to apply the game situations/ strategies to economic behaviour. Mainly, it dwells on two basic situations:

a state of "pure conflict", so that the gains made by one "player" are (he corresponding losses of other(s); and

a state of "mixed conflict and while "players" may cooperate for increasing their pay-off, conflict appears over its division.

Thus, the skipper of a cricket team is very much interested in victory; yet he may be averse to anything which eclipses his own stature vis-à-vis other members 'of the team. However, certain games like chess present a pure conflict situation (ignoring, of course, the many spectator-advisers who may be sitting on either side of the chessboard). Here, player A plans his own strategy for subsequent moves (five, ten, twenty or even more, depending upon his vision) keeping in view the likely counter-moves of the other player B (who may be doing likewise). Who is first able to create a checkmate for the other player would depend on their relative agility along with the viability of strategies. Competing firms in a market may have much to learn from this game situation. Thus, the "discounted price" strategy of one firm may be matched by "competition prize" strategy of another firm.

1.3.4 System Simulation/Monte Carlo Methods: Simulation, in essence, is a "trial and error" (or "suck it and - see") approach which seeks to generate synthetic experience in an artificial universe void the fabulous costs and time dimensions involved in real life experimentation. Actually, in certain situations, it may not be feasible at all to have real life experience (before embarking, on a costly new project). For example, when Indian cosmonauts first entered the spacecraft in 1984, they could not have gone into it with prior real life experience. And, yet, they had to be trained and conditioned to be able to "bear" the first actual experience. Simulation exercises (subjecting the trainees to artificially created stress and strain similar to the one likely to be experienced in a real space voyage) provided an appropriate answer. Likewise, many of the military exercises are conducted in simulated situations; for, a modern war is too costly and destructive a proposition to be initiated merely to provide real, life training. Where sophisticated mathematical analysis is involved, computer simulation may do the trick. It may generate many years of simulated behaviour and history within an hour. The computer output may even represent the behaviour of a firm in its environment.

Thus, alternative decisions/policies may be simulated quickly in order to obtain the best outcome in terms of maximum profit, minimum cost or any 'other criterion. Under system simulation, some type of model "(which suitably reflects the system's operation) is formulated. Interrelationships between the various elements of the system are examined on the basis of predictable behaviour in terms of probability distribution. A series of experiments may be performed on the model of the system. The Monte Carlo method of simulation uses random numbers for solving problems involving a high degree of uncertainty (undermining the feasibility of mathematical formulation). In fact, Monte Carlo methods were first used to resolve gambling problems. It may, however, be kept in view that simulation, too, has its own costs-and limitations.

1.3.5 Statistical Decision Theory: The construction of a pay-off matrix is the crux of the theory. The background for the decision pay-off is built by the decision-making environment, objectives and available "alternatives". Where a manager has to take a sequence of decisions over a span of time (and the alternatives now open are dependent on the options earlier exercised, along with their outcomes), it may be useful to adopt the conceptual approach of decision trees. If the trunk of a tree gets branched off into four sub-trunks (A, B, C, and D) spreading toward East, South, West and North, respectively, a person trying to climb the tree has the initial option of choosing any one of these sub-trunks. But once he has chosen a moving towards East it is presumed that he has closed his other three options of Southward, Westward and Northward movement. So to say, the alternatives available to him are A-1/A-2/A-3/A-4 (and not B-I/ B-2/B-3/B-4, C-1/C-2/C-3/C-4, or D-1/D-2/D-3/D-4).

As applied to a business situation, if a firm says 'no' to a request for price reduction, the alternatives of 5 percent, 10 percent, 15 percent and 20 percent reduction automatically get scored out. In the pay-off matrix under the statistical decision theory, the horizontal rows list alternative decisions that can be made, whereas the vertical columns list the alternative environments or "states of nature" that can be visualized. In this matrix, the "cells" (intersection of a given pair of rows and columns) indicate the outcome of a given combination of decision and environment. The judgment regarding the best alternative may depend on the probabilities of the market behaviour and the desire to fare not too badly even in the 'worst' situation. In a game situation also (where the outcome of a manager's decision depends on the strategies chosen by competitors), a similar pay-off matrix may be constructed,

1.3.6 Inventory Control: There is a local saying that a businessman must always be fully prepared to meet "customer" and "death"; for, any one of these two could appear at any time. This provides the normative basis of some mathematical exercises leading to the construction of inventory models. If the level of customer satisfaction aimed at by a firm is 100 percent (i.e. 'not to say 'no' to any customer appearing at any time and asking for any amount of goods) the inventory (stock of finished goods) required to be maintained may be infinity. At the other extreme, if a businessman does not mind operating (if that operation has any meaning) at zero level of customer satisfaction (or if his total focus is on his own death or on the death of the product), the inventory requirement may be put at just zero. It could be near to in another situation also, i.e., where scheduling and other aspects of planning are so perfect that no idle inventory is maintained anywhere. It is in this context that the art of Japanese management has tried to project "zero-inventory" ("no-inventory") models.

As a practical proposition, it may be more pertinent to observe that the relationship between the "level of customer satisfaction aimed at" and the "level of inventory required" is positive, but a change in the former«tends to call for a more than proportionate change in the hitter. Thus, if a 50 percent level of customer satisfaction can be attained with a stock-in-trade of Rs. 10,000, 60 percent satisfaction would require an inventory of more than Rs. 12,000 (say Rs. 15,000). Mathematical exercises also seek to arrive at the optimum level of various types of inventory to be maintained and the economic order quantity (EOQ), or the economic purchase quantity (EPQ), to be obtained in one lot. The latter exercise is based on a reconciliation of two opposite tendencies. That is, as the size of the lot to be purchased at a time goes up, the carrying costs rise and the procurement costs (per unit) tend to fall.

Assuming a constant rate of use, the average level of .inventory tends to be half the lot-size (EOQ or EPQ). For overall optimum control, ABC analysis may be resorted to. Under the scheme initiated by General Electric, inventory items were divided into three categories: A (vital few/small number with large value); B (middle category/average number with average value); and C (trivial many/large number with small value). Thus, silver may fall in category A, steel in B, and sand in C. The degree of control on thes3 three categories was envisaged in a descending order to avoid the "penny wise, pound foolish1' situation. However, it does not mean that every firm must necessarily have only three categories. Nor is there any sanctity regarding the letters A, B and C. These could as well be X, Y and Z; and such categories could be two, four, five or any other feasible number (above one, since any classification calls for at least two categories).

1.3.7 Econometric Analysis: In a broad sense, it implies the application of mathematical and statistical techniques to economic problems. As such, econometrics is concerned with testing the validity of economic theories, and providing the means of making quantitative predictions (although terms like "econometric theory" and "applied, econometrics" have also come in vogue). The usual modus operandi is to formulate a mathematical model and then to make estimates1 of the parameters in the model through, the application of statistical methods to the best data available. Later on, methods of statistical inference may be applied to conclude whether the hypothesis underlying the model can be rejected or not. In a narrow sense, econometric analysis has often been considered as analogous to demand analysis, since much of the early work in the field concentrated upon the measurement of demand functions, specially, in agriculture. With the appearance of new generations of high-speed computers, econometricians have felt encouraged to build bigger models for measuring relevant relationships for the economy as a whole in several advanced countries. For these exercises, exclusive reliance co. Ltd not be placed on the data obtained from government or trade sources which had to be suitably adjusted, or even scrapped, making it necessary for the econometrician to compile his own data, from primary sources in certain cases. Econometric exercises can be used both for explaining the past behaviour of certain variables (say, the demand for motor cars) and for forecasting the future trends on the basis of the relationships between the quantity demanded, price and income.

1.3.8 Value Analysis: Value analysis may be defined as the application of the techniques of method study to the product design function. It is a procedure which specifies the function of products or components, establishes the appropriate cost, creates alternatives and evaluates them. In this context, the term 'value' implies the least cost for reliably providing the correct function, at the correct time and place, and at a correct standard of quality. Like several other quantitative techniques of modern management, value analysis came to the fore during the Second World War. Pioneering exercises in this regard came from Lawrence D. Miles of the U.S.A. Later, the American Society of Tool and Manufacturing Engineers brought out a comprehensive study entitled "Value Analysis in Manufacturing" (Prentice-Hall, 1967).

Such analysis is of particular relevance to mass manufacturing situations so that even petty gains in production costs can result in sizable overall savings. In this context, the design of a product may be reviewed from time to time. Moreover, efforts may be made to bring about favourable changes in the value ratio (VR). The VR of a product or service may be indicated as the ratio of its worth to its cost for the producer (worth divided by cost) and the ratio of its worth to its price for the customer (worth divided by price). The term "worth" as appearing here if; understood to mean "use plus esteem" for both (the producer and the consumer, again, the term "use," implies the physical power of a product to serve an end, whereas the term "esteem ' connotes the psychological power of a possession which makes it prestigious,

Maruti car released in 1984 by a Government of India undertaking is a case in point. Maruti Udyog Limited (under the able stewardship of its CMD, Mr. V. Krishnamurthy) brought about a drastic departure in design (in collaboration with Japan's Suzuki) from Hindustan Motors Ambassador (whose pedigree could be traced to British Morris) and Premier Automobiles Padmini (still deemed analogous to Italian Fiat). The cost price of Maruti (partly because of the tax concession provided for a smaller car), was only some 60-70 percent of that of the other two cars. As a counter-move, the latter have tried to promote considerations of esteem through their newer models, Contessa and Premier 118-NE (1985). And, considerations of fuel efficiency have affected the designs of almost all automobiles manufactured after 1973, when the oil crises (and the prolonged price hike) assumed dangerous dimensions for the international community.

1.3.9 Capital Budgeting: When some new equipment (fixed asset) is to be acquired, or the feasibility of a new project/as a whole) is being examined, a number of capital budgeting techniques can be employed. Some of these-techniques, like profitability index (PI) or benefit-cost (B/C) ratio, are clearly in the nature of reasoned relationships (ratios) between the present value of benefit (all cash inflows/other socio-economic benefits which can be quantified) and the present value of cost (all cash outflows/other socio-economic costs which can be quantified). If the resultant ratio (benefit divided by cost) is less than one (<1), a project has to be rejected (unless there are overriding political/strategic considerations). Where the ratio is just one (1), the decision-maker can use his discretion (which may usually mean 'no' in the private sector, and a possible "yes" in the public sector). In case the PI or BC ratio is more than one (> 1), the answer is "yes" on the score of viability.

However, in a state of capital rationing, or on account it of time constraint and other administrative/managerial limitations, it may not be feasible to undertake all the projects marked "yes" on the basis of viability criterion. In such a situation, the "cleared" projects can be ranked according to the PI or BC ratio (>l) in a descending order of priority. Somewhat similar is the position when the traditional technique of capital budgeting known as "average (accounting) rate of return" (ARR) is made use of. Here too, the resultant figure (average profit divided by average investment) is a ratio (which may be multiplied by 100 if it is to be expressed as a percentage); and this ratio (percentage) also forms the basis for ranking of projects. However, by itself, it does not throw enough light on the first objective of capital budgeting (to say "yes" or "no to a project).

For that, an expected/reasonable rate of return has to be assumed for the type of project being considered. If the ARR is more than this expected rate, the project is deemed viable (and vice versa) Internal rate of return (IRR), which is a time-adjusted modern method of capital budgeting (indicating the rate of discount/interest at which net present value is zero, i.e., present value of cash inflows equals the present value of cash outflows), also stands in the same position (as ARR). That is, IRR provides basis of ranking, but not of viability as sue which an expected rate of return/interest has to be assumed as a basis of comparison). As against this, the net present value (NPV) method provides a basis both of viability and -of ranking. If the NPV is positive, the project is viable, whereas the greater this positive figure (absolute amount, and not a ratio), the highest is the rank of the particular project. A variant' of NPV is the terminal value method (TVM).

Here, it is presumed that the initial investment on a fixed asset/project is put in a bank account (which fetches interest at the prevailing rate of interest/discount), and that annual cash inflows are reinvested so as to earn compound interest. At the terminal point (when the useful life of the fixed asset/project comes loan end), the total amount (presumed to be) in the bank account is discounted back to the present value at the starting point. If its discounted figure is greater than initial investment, the proposition is considered viable. Given the same rate of interest/discount, the TVM would give the same results as NPV method. There is only a procedural difference. The traditional payback method, however, is basically different. It is not time adjusted, i.e., it ignores the timings of cash flows and, as such, the clement of interest/discount. A project may be deemed viable if the original investment is fully recovered after any number of years.

However, the shorter the payback period, the higher is the

ranking of a project. Thus, various techniques of capital budgeting may give quite different results with regard to both viability and ranking. Moreover, competing projects may not be easily comparable in terms of size of investment, life of project/asset, rate of benefit, total benefit, maintenance/ depreciation, dependability and reliability of forecasts. Further, time adjusted/discounted cash flow (DCF) techniques tend to ignore the element of inflation. If this, too, is taken into account, it would be necessary to have double adjustment/discounting, one for the rate of interest/discount (which, itself, is quite variable) and (he other for changes in the value of money. The latter part (indexation) is an extremely complicated exercise, more so because cash inflows (and even outflows) do not occur at a particular point of time (these being spread over a duration). Indexation, in actual practice, can further fan the fire of inflation, as one may like to learn from the abortive experiment in Brazil.

1.3.10 Replacement Theory: It is applicable to any kind of long-term capital which needs replacement from lime to time. Initially, the theory was applied to physical capital like machines, transport, equipment, railway track and bridges. But, in course of time, its application has been extended to human capital. A big operational research (OR) group of the United Kingdom has developed a "replacement mod" to streamline the pattern of recruitment of new graduates into the group to offset the loss of OR scientists. Another dimension of such a model, particularly for academic/research institutions, maybe to make for proper "time spacing" (staggering) between the intake of exports, in order to ensure fair opportunities for promotion (with a view to avoiding frustration, to which specialists are highly vulnerable).

A further dimension is the tenure of employment along with the age of retirement. Within a few months during the year 1984, the Andhra Pradesh State Government in India reduced the age of retirement from 58 to 55 (obviously, to make room for the unemployed youth), and then again raised it to 53 (possibly to take care of the higher expectation of life, and to provide relief to the inflation-hit old who had yet to fulfil their parental obligations). Here, it is relevant to recount the manner in which these contradictory considerations have been reconciled in Japan: The relationship between the *Zuibatsu* and the system of lifetime employment is an intimate one. Take, for example, Mr. Kagawa, a successful middle-level manager in a major life insurance company in Japan. Mr. Kagawa is now fifty-five and not of the managing director rank, and so must retire. His employer pays him a lump sum separation bonus of US$ 120,000; six times his annual salary of US$ 120,000. But this is not all—the company does not simply say "thank-you and good-bye". Rather, they send Mr. Kagawa to the satellite firm that prints their forms, where he works in a part-time job for the next ten years.

As against this, in the U.S.A., both the business executives and the employing firms seem to prefer frequent/periodical replacement of functionaries. Coming to physical equipment, the replacement theory tries to determine the critical point of time after which the probability of failure would be beyond the tolerance limit. That is, preventive replacement is called for before that date. For example, it may not be safe for a railway train to move on a river bridge whose effective life is over. As against this, if art asset is not usable at all because of a sudden failure (even if the normal span of life is not complete, say as in case of refrigeration/;/air-conditioning it), it is a case of mandatory: replacement. Where there has been a perceptible decline in the-efficiency of a machine, or it has become obsolete with the availability of a much batter machine, discretionary replacement may be called for on the basis of economic reasoning. For example, in 1981, some informal negotiation was initiated for the 'gift'of a 1964-IBM Computer from the Government of India's Planning Commission (New Delhi) to the University of Rajasthan (Jaipur). The University was expected to bear only the dismantling/transport and installation/maintenance costs. Yet, a term of experts advised the University not to adopt a white elephant; instead, they favoured the purchase of a newer generation of mini-computer available at quite a low price (which needs smaller space and costs much less to maintain than the earlier generation large-sized computer).

1.4 Summary

Ratio analysis may be defined to mean "the establishment of a reasoned relationship" of a fixed or variable character-between measurements of certain phenomena having some kind' of linkage. It is not confined to the four walls of financial management. There are vast- and fruitful opportunities for its-application to production (operations), marketing, personnel and general management.

The quantitative approach to management has manifested itself mainly in three forms:

the theory of probability and other branches of statistics;

operations research; and

applications of mathematics to economics, psychology, sociology and other behavioural Studies having their bearing on decision-making, commercial viability or managerial efficacy of various types of entities,

Various factors have added to the significance of quantitative approach in management:

tremendous increase in the quantum of activity;

technological change;

needed fineness in the process of comparison;

need for a capsule or computerized approach;

emphasis on objectivity in decision-making; and

calls for greater conviction through the language of numbers.

Among limitations of the quantitative approach are:

unreal assumptions;

an excuse for not exercising common sense;

vast scope for window-dressing in accounting/

manipulation of financial ratios;

phoney relationships not based on any significant linkage; and

eclipse of qualitative dimensions and individual instances of an extreme character either way (efficiency or inefficiency).

A ratio is comparable to a snapshot taken by a camera at a definite moment. As against this, a fund-flow statement is something like a running reel giving an impression «f movement from one stage to another. Trend analysis (which is like a chain ratio system) can be used to find out the direction and extent/of change. Break-even analysis (including P/V Ratio) is a valuable key to the solution of complex problems in profit planning, specially those relating to multi-product firms.

Questions

1. Ratios are indicators, sometimes pointers, but not in themselves powerful tools of management. In the wrong hands ratios can be very dangerous, as it is easy to draw incorrect conclusions from them, particularly when based on insufficient detailed data. Critically examine this statement with the help of suitable illustrations.
2. What is Network Analysis? Explain and illustrate the differences between PERT and CPM.
3. Suggest a meaningful use of correlation and regression analysis with reference to rainfall and agricultural output in a desert area.
4. What is the relevance of ratio column in simplex matrix applicable to linear programming?
5. How is ratio analysis helpful in inventory control? Present a suitable model relevant to an engineering enterprise.
6. Write short notes on:

   Input-Output Ratios;

   Variance Ratios;

   Value Ratio; and

   Benefit-Cost Ratio.

References

John E. Ullmann , "Theory and Problems of Quantitative Methods in Management (Schaum's Outline Series)," McGraw-Hill Book Company, New York, 1976, p. 106.

Thomas J. Peters and Orbert H. Waterman Jr., "In Search of Excellence—Lessons from America's Best-Run Companies", Harper and Row Publishers, New York, 1982, p. 29. The authors opine: 'The enumerative rationalist approach to management dominates the business schools. It teaches us that well trained professional managers can manage anything. It seeks detached, analytical justification for all decisions. It is right enough to be dangerously wrong, and it has arguably led us seriously astray'.

William G. Ouchi, "Theory Z—How American business can meet: the Japanese challenge," Avon Books, New York (First Avon Printing), April 1982, p. 17.

2

Ratio Pyramid

2.1 The Pyramidical Structure

The word pyramid had its origin in Latin/Greek words “pyramids"/"pyramids", and probably in the Egyptian terra "pir-em-us." As a term of geometry, it stands for any solid figure, the base of which is a polygon whose sides are the bases of triangular surfaces meeting at a common vertex. But, in the context of history, the pyramid typifies any huge structure with a square base and four sloping triangular sides meeting at the top, as those built for royal tombs in ancient Egypt. In fact, the word pyre (Latin/Greek "pyr") means fire or a pile, especially of wood, for burning a corpse in a funeral rite. The structures (piles of wood) usually built for cremation of dead bodies in India look, in a miniature form, like Egyptian pyramids built by piling, from bottom to top, smaller layers over bigger layers of stones.

In commercial parlance, "pyramiding" implies the building up of a structure which enables a smaller top to control a bigger bottom. For example, a "primary holding company" bas controlling interest in certain "intermediate holding companies" which, in turn, plan to have sufficient investment in their own subsidiary companies whose strings can, thus, be indirectly pulled by the primary holding company at the top. As a formal precept, 51 percent (or at least half) of equity ownership is necessary to ensure such control at each stage, so that a parent holding company requires some Rs. 2 crore to control four intermediate holding companies with an equity capital of Rs. 1 crore each (Rs. 4 crore in all). With an investment of Rs. 4 crore, these four intermediate holding companies can control (their own) 16 subsidiary companies having a total equity capital of Rs. 8 crore.

Thus, (even in strict terms), with an investment of Rs. 2 crore, the parent holding company can control the entire pyramidical structure having equity capital of the order of Rs. 14 crore. With an equity-debt ratio of 1:7, it would be possible to control a fortune of Rs. 42 crore just with an investment of Rs. 2 crore (even in strict terms). Informally speaking, if 25 percent equity ownership is effective enough for necessary control, an investment of Rs. 2 crore can control long-term funds amounting to Rs. 126 crore. And, if a compact holding of 10 percent equity capital can serve the purpose, the parent holding company can control assets worth Rs. 666 crore just with an investment of Rs. 2 crore. This "multiplier effect" can be extended still further by increasing the number and/or stages of subsidiary units. The same effect can be attained by gearing up the equity-debt ratio, and/or by reducing thc proportion of investment in equity capital required for controlling a subsidiary unit effectively.

The entire structure of ratio analysis can also be visualized in the form of a pyramid. That is, a series of ratios, at various stages, may be so arranged/depicted in a chart/diagram as to give the appearance of a paramedical figure. At the top may be put the most important ratio indicating, in a way, the end-result of a business, functional area or activity. This can be described as the "primary ratio." Below that may appear certain "secondary .ratios" deemed to be determining constituents of the ratio shown at the top. At the third stage, in this hierarchy, those identifying the precise points of strength/ weakness behind the secondary ratios can be designated as "tertiary ratios." This process of decomposing is capable of being carried down further and further, until the factors leading to success/failure of an enterprise are adequately revealed. Those appearing at the fourth stage can take the form of "subordinate ratios." Likewise, one may think of a series of "descendant ratios1' at the fifth stage (or at still lower levels) in this hierarchy, if the quest for truth makes such exercises imperative (with a view to uncovering the major mysteries of macro-management in micro-situations at minor levels).

2.2 The Primary Ratio

While judging the overall/financial performance of a firm, return on investment (ROI) may be looked upon as tae primary ratio. For private enterprises, ROI is very likely to be the primary focus (even though its maximization may not be deemed advisable for fear of attracting the entry of competing firms, the displeasure of consumers, the wrath of trade unions, and the interference of government through anti-monopoly legislation, progressive taxation and eventual nationalization). Fat even public enterprises may feel compelled, in most situations, to reveal a satisfactory level of ROI (even though they may be combining "social returns'" with "commercial returns" to keep their heads clearly above water). In any case, if ROI is good enough, there may not be much incentive to make deeper probes into levels of efficiency through secondary, tertiary und other ratios at the lower stages of the hierarchy.

The primary ratio can also be a non-financial parameter. For example, in an educational institution, the overall pass percentage of examinees may be looked upon as the primary ratio. If this is very good, not much enquiry is likely to be made with regard to subject-wise or paper-wise results. In case the primary ratio is poor, the authorities as well as the candidates may like to bother themselves even in respect of the awards for every question/assignment and each section/batch of students taught/examined by particular teachers. That is, the process of decomposing may continue downward until the crucial malady spots are discovered. However, a few examinees at the top, and possibly some at the bottom, may always be concerned about minute details (even when 'the overall performance of the university, college or school is quite good).

"What is primary and what is secondary" may as well depend upon the observer's status/angle of vision. Thus, for the

Syndicate/Academic Council/Vice-Chancellor, the pass percentage of the entire University would be the primary ratio. As against this, the pass percentage in a College/Department may be looked upon as the primary ratio by the Principal/Dean or Head/Chairman of the Department concerned.

In certain lines of activity, it may not be feasible to identify any single independent measure as the basic criterion of efficiency. Here, the primary ratio may take the form of a composite/weighted index of a few major criteria (short-listed out of a long inventory of considerations) amenable to quantification. For example, the question may be of judging the performance of police department or, for that matter, of determining if a particular Director-General of Police has been able to deliver the goods during a specific tenure of office. In such a situation, a number of vital positive/negative criteria may be brought to bear to arrive at a primary ratio which appears to be fairly reliable. The negative tally may include the number of cases involving various crimes, like theft and terrorism in relation to the population of the concerned area over a time dimension (as compared to some other area/areas during the same period, or the same area over some other period/periods). The higher the ratio of such crimes, the lower would be the level of police performance.

Taking the positive side of it, the higher the proportion of crimes successfully dealt with (through timely detection, prevention, investigation, punishment etc.), the greater would be the quotient indicating police efficiency. The positive criteria may as well include the help/guidance/education (say, in traffic rules) provided by the police department (on their own) to persons who were in need of the same. The quantitative evaluation of such performance may be difficult; but, it should reflect itself in a decline in the violation of "rules of the road" (or other departures from the norms of discipline as relevant to a social situation). The primary ratio, thus established, may then be decomposed, in several stages, into secondary/tertiary/subordinate/descendant ratios for more and more of minute study, as may be warranted by circumstances, with a view to ascertaining "as to where the shoe really pinches." Variations in the average intensity of a crime and in the social/cultural/economic/political environment may be other vital considerations.

Coming back to the financial domain, the ROI may be worked out as a relationship between operating profit/net profit on the one hand and investment/capital employed on the other. If the former is divided by the latter, the resultant figure would be the return per unit of investment (say one rupee). If it is desired to find out ROI as a percentage, the quotient (just referred to) may be multiplied by 100. It may take the form of a du Pont Chart as given in the chapter on General Management Perspectives.

2.3 Secondary Ratios

If ROI is the primary ratio, its two secondary ratios may be:

a relationship between net profit and sales; and

a relationship between sales and capital employed.

Sometimes alternative terms are used in such equations, such as operating profit for net profit, turnover for sales, and investment for capital employed. When the amount of net profit/operating profit is divided by sales/turnover, and the quotient is multiplied by 100, it indicates the percentage of profit that is being earned on sales. It may be both an indication of business/marketing policy regarding the margin of profit to be sought for and the success of a firm in being able to persuade the customers to buy goods/services at a price which covers a particular margin of profit. Existence of a monopoly situation, market boom, or "skimming price" phase (exploiting the consumer initially, or at a later stage when he has got used to a product/service) may be responsible for high ratio of profit to sales.

Likewise, the prevalence of a competitive situation, market recession, or "penetration price" phase (intentionally charging low, usually in the initial stages, to attract customers and get them away from an established product/firm) may account for a low ratio of profit to sales. A number of public enterprises (and, may be, some cooperative/joint sector/private enterprises also), with a high "social purpose" content may as well be operating at low profit margin, just at break-even (no profit/no loss) level, or even at a loss in certain situations. For example, under a Joint Plan of Operations signed by the Government of India, the WHO and UNICEF, Hindustan Antibiotics (a Government Company) was obliged to produce penicillin "on a non-profit making basis," to maintain its supply for purchase by State/municipal hospitals "for free treatment of patients, particularly women and children," and to provide for "free distribution to children in India."

For arriving at the other secondary ratio, the figure of sales/turnover is divided by the amount of investment/capital employed. The quotient may then be multiplied by 100 to ascertain the percentage. The ratio gives an indication of the rapidity with which capital employed is turned over in the form of sales. That is, if too much capital gets stuck up in top heavy/ underutilized fixed assets/facilities or in-current assets like inventory and receivables, the ratio of sales to investment is likely to be low (indicating poor performance). A less than the required "critical minimum" level of investment, too, may result in the poverty of such a ratio. An outcome of this nature may as well be expected when there is a sudden downswing in the price level, specially of the product(s) sold by the particular firm. On the contrary, inflationary tendencies .may push up the ratio of sales to capital employed (unless the latter is written up under a system of indexation). .

An interesting aspect of these two secondary ratios is their reciprocal character in relation to the primary ratio. That is, so long as the primary ratio remains constant, a change in one of these secondary ratios is fully counterbalanced by a change in the other. So to say, the primary ratio is a product of these two secondary ratios, as indicated below:

(1) $SYR-1 = \frac{Net profit}{Sales}$

(2) $SYR-2 = \frac{Sales}{Capital Employed}$

(3) $PYR = (SYR-1)(SYR-2)$

$$= \frac{Net\ Profit}{Sales} \times \frac{Sales}{Capital Employed}$$

$$= \frac{Net\ Profit}{Capital Employed}$$

Alternatively,

(4) $SYR-1 = \frac{PYR}{SYR-2}$

(5) $SYR-2 = \frac{PYR}{SYR-1}$

2.4 Tertiary Ratios

Tertiary ratios, as secondary to 'secondary ratios', may be used to identify a more precise area of error or weakness/ strength in respect of the activities of an organization. Specific reference may be made to four ratios of a tertiary character, that is:

a relationship between gross profit and sales;

a relationship between overheads and sales;

a relationship between sales and working capital; and

a relationship between sales and fixed assets.

TYR-1 presents the basic postulates regarding profitability in relation to sales as measured by gross profit (i.e., just after deducting direct costs from selling price, but before meeting indirect expenditure/overheads). TYR-2 seeks to project the other side of that picture by focusing attention on office/establishment, selling/marketing and general administration/other overhead costs incurred to support a particular level of sales. It is a measure of managerial efficiency/structural efficacy in an organization. This ratio is likely to be low with "business-like" approach, and high in case of "bureaucratic approach". Of course, all business undertakings are not necessarily business-like in their operations; and, by the same token, every public agency is not necessarily bureaucratic in its demeanour. In most cases, there is a mix of both these attributes in sizable quantum. However, a comparative picture based on the ratio of management expenses to sales/revenue in respect of several similar organizations, or of the same organization over different periods, may be quite revealing. For example, expenses of management in relation to premium income of the Life Insurance Corporation of India (LIC) may be compared with similar ratios of Postal Life Insurance, or with those of several companies operating in the pre-nationalization era for the present ratio for LTC may be compared with its own ratios obtained in earlier years, say prior to 1973, when the Great Inflation had set in.

It may be pertinent to observe that TYR-1 is an arithmetic difference between TYR-1 and TYR-2. This, of course, is subject to the assumption that there is no income of a non-operating character (or, if there is any, the same is not taken into account for the purpose of arriving at the net profit, which is the numerator for arriving at TYR-1). There is also an implicit assumption to the effect that the term "overheads" includes all the expenses which appears against "gross profit" in the profit and loss/income statement. With these assumptions, the following equations may be stated:

1. $$TYR-1=\frac{Gross\,\mathrm{Pr}\,ofit}{Sales}$$

2. $$TYR-2=\frac{Overheads}{Sales}$$

3. $$Net\,\mathrm{Pr}\,ofit=Grossprofit\,\mathrm{min}\,usOverheads$$

4. $$SYR-1=TYR-1\,\mathrm{min}\,usTYR-2$$

$$= \left(\frac{Gross\ Profit}{Sales}\right) \text{minus} \left(\frac{Overheads}{Sales}\right)$$

$$= \frac{Gross profit\ \text{minus}\ Overheads}{Sales}$$

$$= \frac{Net\ Profit}{Sales}$$

Alternatively,

5. $TYR-1 = SYR-1\ plus\ TYR-2$
6. $TYR-2 = TYR-1\ \text{minus}\ SYR-1$

TYR-3 and TYR-4 seek to throw further light on SYR-2 by decomposing the latter into two indicators. Presuming that capital employed is a summation of (gross) working capita (current assets) and fixed assets, the analysis is intended to ascertain which one of these two denominators is having a better impact on the numerator (sales). In negative terms, one may like to know if a poor (low) SYR-2 is attributable (more) to the working capital or to the fixed assets. Flaws like sluggishness, overinvestment, and inefficient management of working capital/current assets and/or fixed assets may be discovered through such introspection. Some firms, either ab initio or through passage of time, maybe in a state of underutilization of working capital and/or fixed capital. In other words, the amount of sales may not be commensurate with (adequate for) a particular level of investment, say in inventory/other constituents of working capital or machinery/other constituents of fixed capital. This may be judged on the basis of certain norms of expectations with reference to particular types of activities/areas. These norms, in their turn, may be based on the relevant tertiary ratios (TYR-3 and TYR-4) obtaining in other firms, or in the same firm during earlier accounting periods (at other points of time).

The nature of relationship between TYR-3 and TYR-4 (complementarily of the denominator) is different from that found between TYR-1 and TYR-2 (complementarily of the numerator). As such, different sets of equations, as noted below, have to be devised for depicting this different kind of relationship between TYR-3 and TYR-4 (in the context of SYR-2):

1. $$TYR-3=\frac{Sales}{WorkingCapital}$$

2. $$TYR-4=\frac{Sales}{FixedAssets}$$

3. Capital Employed = Working capital + Fixed capital plus Fixed asset
4. SYR -2 = Reciprocal of (Reciprocal of TYR -3 plus Reciprocal of TYR – 4)

=Reciprocal of $\left(\frac{WorkingCapital}{Sales}+\frac{FixedAssets}{Sales}\right)$

=Reciprocal of $\frac{CapitalEmployed}{Sales}$

$$=\frac{Sales}{CapitalEmployed}$$

Alternatively,

5. TYR -3 = Reciprocal of (Reciprocal of SYR 2 minus Reciprocal of TYR-4) =Reciprocal of

$$=\left(\frac{CapitalEmployed}{Sales}\min us\frac{FixedAssets}{Sales}\right)$$

= Reciprocal of $\frac{WorkingCapital}{Sales}$

$$=\frac{Sales}{WorkingCapital}$$

6. TYR -4 = Reciprocal of (Reciprocal of SYR – 2 minus Reciprocal of TYR – 3) = Reciprocal of

$$\left(\frac{CapitalEmployed}{Sales} \min us \frac{WorkingCapital}{Sales}\right)$$

$$=\text{Reciprocal of } \frac{FixedAssets}{Sales} = \frac{Sales}{FixedAssets}$$

Further,

7. If TYR -3 > twice SYR -2,
   It means that Working Capital has more positive relationship with Sales (and that working capital is less than Fixed Assets).
8. If TYR- 4> twice SYR-2,
   It means that Fixed Assets have more positive relationship with Sales (and that Fixed assets are less than Working Capital).
9. If TYR- 3 = twice SYR-2,
   then TYR-4 = twice SYR-2,
   and TYR -3 = TYR -4;
   also Working Capital = Fixed Assets,
   and SYR 2 = $\frac{TYR-3 plus TYR-4}{4}$

2.5 Subordinate Ratios

For each one of the tertiary, there might be several subordinate ratios serving to make a deeper probe into the weakness/strength of an organization. Thus, if there are two ratios subordinate to each tertiary ratio, one could think of eight subordinate ratios in all. But, there is no sanctity with two us a number/multiplier. Thus, if three ratios are subordinate to one tertiary ratio (and the number of tertiary ratios is maintained at four), there might be twelve subordinate ratio in all. In fact it is not necessary that for every tertiary ratio an equivalent number of subordinate ratios be worked out. One tertiary ratio may have two subordinate ratios, another one may have three, a third one may have four, while the fourth one may have five (so that there are 14 subordinate ratios in all). Further, all these subordinate ratios may not be equally important, and a firm is quite free to work out only so many of these as are pertinent to a particular situation or point of time.

As a case in point, the ratio of sales to working capital (TYR-3) may be decomposed into three subordinate ratios:

ratio of sales to cash (SER-1);

ratio of sales to stock/inventory (SER-2); and

ratio of sales to debtors/receivables (SER-3).

The presumption is that cash, inventory and receivables are the three (main) constituents of working capital. In case there are other constituents (deemed important), say short-term investments and prepaid expenses on the assets side of a Balance Sheet, more subordinate ratios (beyond three referred to above) can be worked out. If the term working capital is interpreted to mean "net working capital" (current assets minus current liabilities), the relationship of sales with trade creditors/bills payable/other current liabilities may as well be identified. This would, of course, make the exercise more complicated; for, the ratio of sales to payables (SER-4) would call for a 'deduction process' as against the 'aggregation process' applicable to SER-1, SER-2, and SER-3 for arriving at TYR-3.

Likewise, subordinate ratios relevant to other tertiary ratios can also be thought of. For example, TYR-4 (ratio of sales to fixed assets) maybe decomposed into several subordinate ratios (SERs) like:

ratio of sales to land and buildings;

ratio of sales to plant and machinery; and

ratio of sales to other fixed assets.

No doubt, all these three subordinate ratios may not be equally significant; maybe, most firms find plant and machinery as the most relevant denominator. Similarly, TYR-2 (ratio of overheads to sales) may be decomposed into several sub-ordinate ratios, (SERs) like:

ratio of factory overheads to sales;

ratio of office overheads to sales; and

ratio of marketing overheads to sales.

Such a functional decomposition may not be feasible in respect of TYR-1 (ratio of gross profit to sales).

However, in case of multi-product firms, an attempt may be made to identify the gross profit earned on each line of production separately. Maybe, in this process, the firm finds that a particular product or department is showing (gross) loss. No doubt, such an exercise may not be operationally feasible in many situations. Moreover, it may call for, besides the decomposition of numerator (gross profit), a decomposition of the denominator also (sales). As such, the type of algebraic relationship found to exist between the several ratios subordinate to a particular tertiary ratio may not be found to subsist, even if these (independently worked out) SERs tell some useful story of comparative efficiency within a particular firm. Alternatively, one may like to distinguish between "operating profit" and "non-operating profit". The former is supposed to emerge from the main operation(s) of a firm, whereas the latter ma-y appear as a consequence of some accidental/side activities (like a textile mill earning some rent for the use of its assembly hall by an outside party on a particular day for an activity not connected with the business of the mill). However, such a decomposition may appear more appropriate at the TYR level (calling for the construction of another tertiary ratio). Further, a relationship between non-operating profit and sales may not be strictly pertinent.

2.6 Descendant Ratios

Descending further down to the base of "ratio pyramid", it may be possible to think of a number of descendant ratios (DERs) in respect of a particular' subordinate ratio (SER). Thus, SER-1 (ratio of sales to cash) may be decomposed into:

ratio of sales to cash in hand; and

ratio of sales to cash at bank.

Likewise, SER-3 (ratio of sales to receivables) may be decomposed into:

ratio of sales to book debts; and

ratio of sales to bills receivable.

This is based on the presumption that the concerned firm makes a distinction between those receivable which are in the form of hundis/bills of exchange and other book debts (arising through credit sales, but not supported/evidenced by such negotiable documents).

By the same token, SER-4 (ratio of sales to payables) can be subdivided into two ratios:

ratio of sales to trade creditors; and

ratio of sales to bills payables. .

In case SER-4 covers other current liabilities also, a third descendant ratio (DER) may as well be worked out in respect thereof (that is, ratio of sales to other current liabilities). On the other hand, if the firm concerned does not observe any distinction between trade creditors and bills payable, the first two descendant ratios in respect of SER-4 may be combined into one DER only (the other DER being in respect of other current liabilities). In case trade creditors and bills payable constitute a single category, and other liabilities do not exist, SER-4 may not have any DER at all.

The decomposition of SER-2 (ratio of sales to inventory) may be dealt with in some detail. SER-2 may be sub-divided into (say) three descendant ratios:

ratio of sale$ to raw materials (DER-1);

ratio of sales to goods-in,-process (DER-2); and

ratio of sales to finished goods (DER-3)

The following may be framed in its connection.

Inventory=Raw Materials plus Goods-in-process plus Finished Goods

$$DER-1=\frac{Sales}{RawMaterials}$$

$$DER-2=\frac{Sales}{Goods-in-\Pr ocess}$$

$$DER-3=\frac{Sales}{FinishedGoods}$$

SER-2 = Reciprocal of (Reciprocal of DER -1 plus Reciprocal of DER-2 plus Reciprocal of DER-3)

=Reciprocal of

$$\left(\frac{RawMaterials}{Sales}+\frac{Goods-in-process}{Sales}+\frac{FinishedGoods}{Sales}\right)$$

$$= \text{Reciprocal of } \frac{Inventory}{Sales}$$

$$=\frac{Sales}{Inventory}$$

Alternatively,

DER-1 = Reciprocal of (Reciprocal of SER -2 minus Reciprocal of DER -2 minus Reciprocal of DER -3)

=Reciprocal of

$$\left(\frac{Inventory}{Sales}-\frac{Goods-in-process}{Sales}-\frac{FinishedGoods}{Sales}\right)$$

=Reciprocal of

$$=\frac{Sales}{RawMaterials}$$

DER-2=Reciprocal of (Reciprocal of SER -2 minus Reciprocal of DER-1 minus Reciprocal of DER-3)

=Reciprocal of

$$\left(\frac{Inventory}{Sales}-\frac{RawMaterials}{Sales}-\frac{FinishedGoods}{Sales}\right)$$

=Reciprocal of

$$=\frac{Sales}{Goods-in-process}$$

SER-3 = Reciprocal of (Reciprocal of SER-2 minus Reciprocal of DER -1 minus Reciprocal of DER-2)

=Reciprocal of

$$\left(\frac{Inventory}{Sales}-\frac{RawMaterials}{Sales}-\frac{Good-in-process}{Sales}\right)$$

$$=\text{Reciprocal of } \frac{FinishedGoods}{Sales}=\frac{Sales}{FinishedGoods}$$

2.7 The Size of the Pyramid

Above in this chapter have been discussed five generations of ratios, starting from PYR (primary ratio) at the top, followed by SYRs (secondary ratios), TYRs (ternary ratios), SERs (subordinate ratios), and DERs (descendant ratios) at the bottom/base of the pyramid. This pedigree can be carried down to still lower levels, if such an extension of enquiry (say, as regards the ratio of sales to various types of raw materials, generation, which can be given any other name) is deemed purposeful. Likewise, the number of generations in this focus may be reduced from five to four, three or two (but not less than two; for, in that case, the pyramid would cease to exist), The lowest generation (whatever it may be) is called the base which, in that sense, is an adjustable one (unlike the stone pyramids, which had a fixed base, and which could be extended only upward of that state of technology).

The overall size of a ratio pyramid would be determined by two variables, viz. the number of generations in the pedigree, and the number of branches in each generation. And. in actual practice, the number of branches (ratios) at various levels (generations) need not be uniform (just as there may be no uniformity with regard to number of sub-trunks, branches, sub-branches, leaves, etc. in a tree). In fact, many trees can be thought of as pyramids upside down. As such, there is much of resemblance between a family tree (pedigree of successive generations) and a ratio pyramid. The two main determinants of the size of family (whether of individuals or of ratios) would be the same in either case.

Assuming that there are five generations and that subdivision at each level (following PYR at the top) takes place in multiples of three, the total number of ratios in the resultant pyramid would be 12.1. Since there is only one ratio at the top, the following equation can be framed.

$F=1 + M^1 4- M^2 + \dots M$

Where

F stands for family size (total number of members in the family)

M stands for the multiplier (number of branches emerging at each stage, taken to be uniform to facilitate algebraic treatment), and

N stands for the number of generations (pedigree) in focus after 1 (the primary ratio or head of the family)

As much

$F = 1 + 3^1 + 3^2 + 3^3 + 3^4$

$= 1 + 3 + 9 + 27+81$

$= 121$

2.8 Partial versus Total View of the Situation

Economic administration and financial management had attained a high state of perfection in ancient India, as evidenced by Kautilya's Arthashastra written more than two thousand years back (even before the dawn of Christian era). However, financial summaries of the Western style have a history of some six hundred years only. The partners Francesco di Marco da Prata and Domenico di Cambio are reported to have drawn up a detailed statement of assets and liabilities on August 30, 1389, quite in the modern manner. Specific instructions for the preparation of a summary (or "inventory" as then christened) were given by Lucas Pacioli, believed to be the author of the first published accounting treatise (1494). Johann Gotlieb's treatise, appearing half a century later (Niirnberg, 1546), illustrated the "balancing account" which continued in use, as a standard book-keeping practice, until the nineteenth century. This was an integral part of the ledger into which balances of asset and liability accounts were closed in a manner similar to the contemporary practice of closing the income and expense accounts into a summary account. After a quarter century (1574), the Mines Royal, being in financial difficulties because of a business depression, made a statement entitled "An Estimate of the Stock remaining at the Mines and the value thereof at Christmas last" (a mere enumeration of assets without referencc to liabilities), for the benefit of its stockholders.

The large-scale use of financial statements, as bases of opinions regarding the desirability of extending bank credit, it may be said to have been initiated on February 9, 1895, when the Executive Council of the New York State Bankers' Association adopted a resolution to recommend to the members of this association that they request borrowers of money from their respective institutions to give them written statements over their signatures of thcir assets and liabilities, in such form as the Committee on Uniform Statements of the various groups recommend. This gave currency to "property-statement blanks" as an indication of the applicant's solvency in the context of his financial responsibility. Ratios, as a basis for bank credit, had come into use by 1908, when a writer ruled: "Credit is usually extended on the strength of quick assets, and many good judges feel that the ratio of quick assets to liabilities should be about 2 to 1," (William M. Rosendale in Bankers' Magazine, Vol. 78). In course of time, this norm of quick ratio was brought down to 1:1, whereas that of current ratio was pushed up to 2:1 from the earlier stipulation of 1:1 made by Thomas F. Woodlock (author of The Anatomy of a Railroad Report, 1900) in somewhat vague terms: "In general, current items on each side of the account should at least fairly offset each other, year by year." Woodlock had also referred to "the percentage of operating expenses to gross earnings" (later named as "operating ratio" by Lawrence Chamberlain in 1 he Principles of Bond Investment, 1911) and certain other relationships like "the ratio of fixed charges to net income", and "the relative proportion which funded debt and stock of a company should bear the actual cost of the property". While using the ratio of transportation expenses to operating revenues, Lawrence Chamberlain called it "transportation ratio".

At the same time, he described the ratio of margin of profit to total net income as the "factor of safety". In a way, Lawrence Chamberlain also initiated the “total versus partial view” approach, though he did not use this terminology. He tried to find out the relationships of various components of an item to the whole in the special context of railroads, such as "the proportion of various revenues to total operating revenues" and "the proportion of various expenses to total operating expenses". Later on, this technique got known as "common-size" or "100 percent" statement.

The same (partial versus total view) approach was echoed a little later, in 1913, by F.B. Snyder (Bankers' Magazine, Volume 86) in the context of bank credit. The writer revolted against the supremacy of current ratio as the basic criterion, and raised questions regarding the reasonable proportion of cash to liabilities, goods on hand to annual sales, arid receivables to credit sales (later on, known as "debtors ratio"). A few years later, Alexander Wall's article "Study of Credit Barometrics" (Federal Reserve Bulletin, March 1919) appeared as a landmark in the presentation of a system of analysis of financial statements by means of ratios. Wall's ideas took the form of several books, including the one entitled "Ratio Analysis of Financial Statements" (in collaboration with Raymond W. Tuning) published in 1928 (Harper and Bros., 'New York), The thesis developed by Alexander Wall was that, in order to have a, complete picture, relationships in financial statements other than that of current asset to current liabilities should also be considered (as necessary checks on the current ratio). Some of those who read these writings began to visualize ratio analysis as a magic touchstone for infallible judgment, or as an oracle for sure success in business.

Support had also been lent to this view by James H. Bliss

while stating in the preface to a book (1923). In every branch of industry there are certain characteristic financial and operating ratios, depending upon the nature of its activities. Bliss added that such ratios might be determined by averaging the ratios of the concerns in the industry and, to "enjoy the average measure of success", a concern must approximate to these ratios. This was an attempt to establish "standard ratios" for specific categories of business enterprises. However, two sets of doubts followed in this regard: first, whether there could be any rule-of-thumb standard in respect of business ratios (like the norm of human body temperature which, too, has a margin of variation); and, secondly ranting the feasibility of such a standard), whether any average (say, arithmetic mean, median or mode) of the ratios obtaining in existing enterprises would be necessarily desirable and reliable enough as a guide.

Serious criticism of ratio analysis appeared in print Bas early as 1925. Stephen Oilman raised four objections in this regard. First, a change in a ratio can be interpreted only in the light of the changes in each of the two variables the relationship of which it represents (like a large-scale acquisition of certain imported/controlled raw materials suddenly pushing down DER-1, SER-2 and TYR-3, even when sales have not declined). Secondly, it is difficult to comprehend the connection of a ratio with the balance sheet (or other financial statement) from which it is computed (as it may not be possible to write back a Balance Sheet on the basis of certain ratios). Thirdly, the ratios give an unwanted impression of finality (for, these could easily be the prophets of doom). Fourthly, the ratios do not give a comprehensive view of the balance sheet relationships (since only some isolated items therein are taken into account). However, a study published in 1935 found that failing firms exhibit significantly different ratio measurements than continuing entities. Several such studies had appeared by 1967.7

Some of these points were re-echoed later by Edward I.

Altman who wrote in the very beginning of an epoch-making paper (1968), "Academicians seem to be moving toward the elimination of ratio analysis as an analytical technique in assessing the performance of the business enterprise. Theorists downgrade arbitrary rules of thumb, such as company ratio comparisons, widely used by practitioners. Since attacks on the relevance of ratio analysis emanate from many esteemed members of the scholarly world, does this mean that ratio analysis is limited to the world of "nuts and bolts"? Or, has the significance of such an approach been unattractively garbed and therefore unfairly handicapped? Can we bridge the gap, rather than sever the link, between traditional ratio "analysis" and the more rigorous statistical techniques which have become popular among academicians in recent years".

Altman developed a model for multiple discriminant analysis (MDA) as a statistical technique for classifying observations into one of several a priori groupings depending upon the observation's individual characteristics. MDA was an adaptation from biological and behavioural sciences into the domain of financial analysis. Its first application was reported to have been made by R.A. Fisher in "The Use of Multiple Measurements in Taxonomic Problems" (Annals of Eugenics, No. 7, September 1936), and more pertinently (nearer the finance area) by D.D. Durand in "Risk Elements in Consumer Instalment Financing" (National Bureau of Economic Research, New York, 1941). These writings were followed by I.E. Walter's highly relevant paper entitled "A Discriminant Function for Earnings Price Ratios of Large Industrial Corporations" (Review of Economics and Statistics, Vol. XLI, February 1959) and K.V. Smith's technical study on "Classification of Investment Securities Using MDA" (Institute Paper No. 101, Purdue University, Institute for Research in the Behavioural, Economic and Management Sciences, 1965).

Altman (1968) opined that ratio analysis presented in, univariate fashion was susceptible to faulty interpretation and potential confusion. For instance, nothing may appear serious so long as a firm has "above average liquidity" whereas it may be potentially bankrupt with poor profitability. As against this, multivariate analysis is an attempt toward studying a full(er) profile of any entity. Even the judges, in beauty contests, are no longer prepared to confer titles like "Miss Universe" and "Miss World" merely on the basis of (a subjective/partial reading of) facial features; rather, a computerized result (based on wide-ranging/objective scores) is sought to be produced (for the fuller satisfaction of competitors and their fans). In a somewhat similar fashion, MDA attempts to derive a linear "combination" of relevant characteristics which best discriminate between the groups in focus (such as solvent or healthy and insolvent or sick). Discriminating coefficients, when applied to actual ratios, as a basis for classification of various entities into any one of the mutually exclusive groups (that is, each firm appears in some category, and no firm appears in more than one category). Individual variable values are transformed into a single discriminant score (or Z value, as Altman calls it) which is then used to classify the units under study.

In Altman's MDA model, Z is a weighted index of a small group of five (liquidity, profitability, leverage, solvency, and activity) ratios, chosen on the basis of:

Observation of the statistical significance of various alternative functions including determination of the relative contribution of each independent variable;

Evaluation of inter-correlations between the relevant variables;

Observation of the predictive accuracy of the various profiles; and

Judgment of the analyst.

The choice was made out of 22 "original" ratios, after evaluation of the "contribution of the entire profile". Acceding to Altman, since this process is essentially iterative, there is no claim regarding the optimally of the resulting discriminant function; this, however, does the best job among the alternatives which included numerous computer runs analyzing different ratio-profiles. On an application of the "F" test (relating the difference between the average values of the ratio in each group to the variability or spread of values of the ratios within each group, i.e., bankrupt and non-bankrupt), it was found that variables X1, X2, X3 and X4 were all significant at .001 level, whereas variable X5 did not show a significant difference between groups. The last one was the second most weighted ratio in terms of relative contribution as observed in a scaled vector computed by multiplying corresponding elements by the square roots of the diagonal elements of the variance co-variance matrix. The resultant composition of the Altman model is given in Table 2.1.

Table 2.1: Relative Contribution of the Variables

Variable	Scaled Vector	Ranking
X1	3.29	5
X2	6.04	4
X3	9.89	1
X4	7.42	3
X5	5.41	2

Altman came to the conclusion that, with Z>2.99 a firm could be placed in the non-bankrupt group, whereas a firm having Z<2.99 would be classed as bankrupt. Accordingly, a score between 1.81 and' 2.99 might represent "zone of ignorance" or "gray area" where misclassification can be observed for which may represent temporary sickness/a state of transition from one group to another). The predictive accuracy of the MDA Model (Initial Sample) adopted by Altman was as high as 95 percent one year prior to actual bankruptcy but the same was found to fall sharply to 72 percent (two years prior), l 48 percent (three years prior), and 29 percent (four years prior), before rising surprisingly to 36 percent (five years prior to actual bankruptcy). Thus, it was a real "hit or miss" at the other end. All of the observed ratios revealed a deteriorating trend as bankruptcy approached, though the last one (X5) was somewhat sticky (not quite sensitive). The most serious change in the majority of these ratios was found to occur between the third and second year prior to actual bankruptcy. Besides X5 to V5, the current ratio, too, suffered a serious decline about this time ('although, otherwise, its fall was neither so consistent nor so steep). The Beaver study (1966-1967) had concluded that the "cash flow to debt ratio" was the best single ratio for prediction. This ratio was not considered by Altman (1968) who claimed superiority, of his results over those obtained by Beaver (whose analysis, as indicated, showed firms exhibiting failure tendencies as much as five years prior to the actual failure)

Edward Deakin in "A Discriminant Analysis of Predictors of Failure", Journal of Accounting Research, Vol. 10, Spring 1972 and Marc Blum "Failing Company Discriminant Analysis," Journal of Accounting Research, Vol. 12, Autumn 1974 tried to improve upon Altman's model. Deakin's original model included as many as fourteen variables; these were reduced to only five variables in the revised model (1972). One of these was the current ratio, whereas another one was the ratio of cash to total assets. The denominator of Altman's X5 was changed from total assets to current, assets (as a more reliable basis for studying the relationship with sales). For net income, however, total assets continued to be the denominator (as in Altman's model). Both Altman and Deakin derived their models from a statistical search procedure for the "best" function without much logical support as such. Relationships which were not causal as such could, at any time, turn out to be spurious. For example, a statistician might have perceived that prices of potatoes and onions 'were about the same (say, two rupees per kilogram) over a certain period in a certain city (say, Jaipur). But that alone would not entitle him to declare that a ratio of 1:1 is the best function. However, Deakin and Blum did succeed, statistically, in achieving greater predictive accuracy (than Altman) several years before bankruptcy. Blum's model (1974) was based on the following twelve variables:

I. Liquidity

(A) Short-run Flow

(1) The "quick flow" ratio.

(2) Ratio of net quick assets to inventory.

(B) Long-run flow

(3) Ratio of cash flow to total liabilities.

(4) Ratio of net worth at fair market values to total liabilities.

(5) Ratio of net worth at book value to total liabilities.

II. Profitability

(6) Rate of return to common stock holders who invest for a minimum of three years.

III. Variability and Trend

(7) Standard deviation of net income over a period.

(8) Trend "breaks" for net income.

(9) Slope for net income.

(10) Standard deviation, trend breaks and slope of net quick assets to inventory ratio.

Blum's complicated model (1974) appears to have inhibited its use. On the other hand, Altman's relatively simple model (1968) has been adopted in toto by several writers, such as: (i) L.V.L.N. Sharma and G.B. Rao, "Financial Ratios as Predictors of Failure: A Multivariate Approach" (Indian Manager, April-June 1976); and (ii) K.M. Pande and CD. Bhattacharya, "Corporate Financial Strength: Application of Multi-Discriminant Analysis" (Jodhpur Management Journal, Vol. 3). About the same time, Jarrod W. Wilcox built up another (apparently simple) model in "The Gambler's Ruin Approach to Business Risk" (Shan Management Review, Vol. 18, Fall 1976). This model assumed that, at any time, a firm's financial state can be defined by its "adjusted cash position" or "net liquidation value" (liquidation value of assets less the liquidation value of debts).

According to Wilcox (1976), the liquidation value (LV)

changes from year to year through inflows and outflows and the change in financial state takes place always by a fixed amount ("size of the bet" or $), Thus, if the probability of the firm gaining the bet is p, and that of its losing the bet is q, then unless p>q, the firm is bound to fail. The length of period up to the time of actual failure is determined by the size of the firm's net liquidation value in combination with the size and probabilities of inflows and outflows of liquid resources. WiJcox's model (1976) was an attempt to identify "reserve strength" of a firm on the basis of the following (rather arbitrary) assumptions regarding liquidation value (Table 2.2).

Table 2.2: Liquidation Value (Percentage)

Cash Equivalents	100
Other Current Assets	70
Long-Term Assets	50
Debt	100

L.C. Gupta (1983), not convinced that "more "complicated always means better," adopted Beaver's idea (1966-1967), carried it further and tried to adapt the same to the Indian situation. In this process, a long list of some 56 ratios was furnished. Thereafter, L.C. Gupta (1983) tried to define the analytical techniques for real world conditions by identifying the following five "best" ratios which, as he claimed, show fairly good agreement among themselves in the classification achieved (except some borderline cases).

Ratio of EBDIT to "Sales (net of excise)," R-1;

Ratio of OCF to "Sales (net of excise)," R-9;

Ratio of EBDIT to "total assets plus accumulated depreciation," R-3;

Ratio of OCF to "total assets plus accumulated depreciation," R-I1; and

Ratio of OCFto "interest plus 0.25 of Debt," R-4.

N.B, EBDIT stands for earnings before-depreciation-interest-and-taxation. OCF implies operating cash flow (earnings-after-interest-and-taxation, with depreciation provision added back).

Taking 0.25 of outstanding debt (indicating-the amount of pre-tax earnings, at 50 percent tax rate, needed for repayment) implies an eight-year repayment period.

Analysis of the diagram representation depicts that thc bigger circle represents the total area/coverage (both sick and non-sick companies). The three smaller circles (A, B and C) represent, on the basis of three crucial ratios, the area of companies likely to fall into the category of sick units. The number of these smaller circles can be varied (say, two, four or five); but, there cannot be any "union of ratio sets" unless there are at least two inner circles (ratios). With only one ratio as the basis, quite a big arcs (in A, B and C) might be predicted as sick. Then, there are overlapping areas between two circles (A and B, B and C, and C and A). Here, sickness can be predicted with greater certainty. Finally, there is some (small) overlapping area between all the three circles (A, B and C). This can be called as one of "definite" sickness (if the guiding ratios are at all worth the salt).

2.9 Summary

In commercial parlance, "pyramiding" implies the building up of a structure which enables a smaller top to control a bigger bottom. The entire structure of ratio analysis can also be visualized in the form of a pyramid. At the top may be put the most important ratio indicating the end-result of an activity. This may be described as the 'primary ratio' (PYR), say return on investment (ROI). The primary ratio can also be a non-financial parameter, such as the overall pass percentage of examinees in an educational institution.

In certain lines of activity, it may not be feasible to identify any single independent measure as the basic criterion of efficiency. Here, the primary ratio may take the form of a composite index based on a few major criteria. These may be positive or negative. While judging the performance of the police department, the negative tally may cover the number and intensity of crimes. On the positive side may appear the crimes successfully dealt with, as also the guidance and education provided by the police department.

If ROI is the primary ratio, its secondary ratios (SYR) may be:

a relationship between net profit and sales; and a relationship between sales and capital employed.

Tertiary ratios (TYRs), secondary to secondary ratios, may cover:

a relationship between gross profit and sales;

a relationship between overheads and sales;

a relationship between sales and working capital; and

a relationship between sales and fixed assets.

For each one of the tertiary ratios, there might be several subordinate ratios (SERs), such as (with reference to TYR-3):

ratio of sales to cash;

ratio of sales to inventory; and

ratio of sales to receivables.

Descending further down to the base of ratio pyramid, it may be possible to think of a number of descendant ratios" (DERs) in respect of a particular subordinate ratio. Thus, SER-2 may be decomposed into:

1. ratio of sales to raw materials;
2. ratio of sales to goods-in-process; and
3. ratio of sales to finished goods.

Questions

1. 'Some have argued that traditional ratio analysis is no longer an important analytical technique in the academic environment due to (he relatively unsophisticated manner in which it has been presented. Altman's point is that ratios, if analyzed within a multivariate framework, will take on a greater statistical significance than the standard techniques of ratio comparison (Brigham and Johnson,

"Issues in Managerial Finance", The Dryden Press, 1976). Discuss this statement and give your own views on Financial Ratios and Multiple Discriminate Analysis an presented by Edward i. Altman (Journal of Finance, September 1968).

2. Construct a three-stage Ratio Pyramid comprising the Primary Ratio, Secondary Ratios and Tertiary Ratios as applicable to hospital management.
3. Depict a five-stage Ratio Pyramid comprising PYR, SYRs, TRYs, SERs, and DERs to ascertain (he financial status of a sick cotton textiles mill seeking to secure a loan from a commercial bank.
4. If the ratio of Net Profit to Sales (SYR-1) is 0.25 (25 percent) and the ratio of Sales to Capital Employed (SYR-2) is 0,80 (80 percent) the ratio of Net Profit to Capital Employed (PYR) would be;
5. If PYR is 0.30 (30 percent), and is SYR-1 isU60 (60 percent), SYR-2 would be:
   2.00 (200 percent);
   0.90 (90 percent);
   0.50 (50 percent); or
   none of the above.
6. If the ratio of Gross Profit to Sales (TYR-1) is 0.45, and the ratio of Overheads to Sales (TYR-1) is 0.18 (18 percent), SYR-1 would be:
   0.081 (8.1 percent);
   0.27 (27 percent);
   0.63 (63 percent);
   none of the above.
7. 7. If SYR-1 is 0.33 (33 percent), and TYR-2 is 0.22 (22 percent), TRY-I would be:
   0.55 (55 percent)
   0.11 (11 percent)
   0.0726 (7.26 percent)
   none of the above.
8. If the ratio of Sales to Working Capital (TYR-3) is 10.0,

and the ratio of Sales to Fixed Assets (TYR-4) is 2.5, SYR-2 would be

12.5

7.5

4.0

2.0

9. Explain and illustrate "Ratio Sets" in the context of "Partial versus Total View" regarding the soundness of a business entity.
10. Write short notes on:

Operating Ratio;

Factor of Safety;

Predictors of Failure; and

Gambler's Ruin Approach.

References

Edward I. Altman, "Financial Ratios, Discriminate Analysis and the Prediction of Corporate Bankruptcy" (Journal of Finance, September 1968) in Eugene F. Brigham and Ramon E. Johnson (Eds.), "Issues in Managerial Finance," The Dryden Pres*, Hinsdale, Illinois, 1976, pp. 22-23).

James H- Bliss, "Financial'. and Operating Ratios in Management," The Ronald Press Co., New York, 1923.

John N. Myer," Financial Statement Analysis," Prentice-Hall, Inc., Englewood Cliffs, New Jersey, 1969, page 4 (based on Enrico Bensa's "Francesco de Marco .da Praia," Fratelli Treves, Milan, 1928, pp. 414-17). Myer's book was first published in 1939.

L.C. Gupta, "Financial! Ratios for Monitoring Corporate Sickness-Towards a More Systematic Approach," Oxford University Press, Delhi (Bombay/Calcutta/Madras), 1983.

Lucas Piicioli, "Suha dc Arithmetical' Section IX, Treatise XI, Chapters II and III, Venice, 1494.

Manmohan S. Kumar, "Growth, Acquisition and Investment (An analysis Of the growth of industrial firms and their overseas activities)," Occasional Paper 56, Cambridge University Press, 1984.

R.F. Smith and A.H. Winakor, "Changes in the Financial Structure of

Unsuccessful Corporations," University of Illinois, Bureau of Business Research, 1935; (b) W.B. Hickman, "Corporate Bond Quality and Investor Experience", Princeton University Press, 1958; (c) W.H. Beaver, "Financial Ratios as Predictors of Failure," Empirical Research in Accounting, Selected Studies, 19(>6 (Institute of Professional Accounting, January 1967), and (M. Kumari, "Financial Radios as a Means of Forecasting]bankruptcy," 'Management International Review, Vol. 4, 1966.

Stephen Oilman, "Analyzing Financial Statements," The Ronald Press Co., New York, 1925 (revised edition, 1934).

3

Financial Management Ratios

3.1 Liquidity Ratios

Having viewed the hierarchical structure of a ratio pyramid, it is, now proposed to study ratios in the context of their functional classification. Since finance was the first area which saw the application of ratio analysis to modern management, it would be in the fitness of things to start with a discussion of financial management ratios. Within the broad domain of finance, the "ratio technique," as such, would appear to have first unfolded itself in the study of "liquidity position" of borrowing firms at the hands of commercial banks. The sheet anchor of this scrutiny was the relationship between current assets and current liabilities (what came to be known as the "current ratio").

The word "liquid" has had French/Latin origin in "liquids" (fluid) and "liqueur" (to make fluid). In physical sciences, the term is used for a substance which can flow freely in juxtaposition to something "solid". According to The Penguin Dictionary of Economics (1980), "An asset is liquid if it is CASH or can be quickly converted into cash at little loss. Assets are said to possess degrees of Liquidity which are their nearness to cash." That is, liquidity is the ease with which an asset can be exchanged for money, and the liquidity of an asset is determined by the nadir of market on which it is traded. Thus, an investment in the shares of a joint stock company listed/quoted on the stock exchange may be more liquid than house property which (normally) cannot be sold so readily every when the demand for houses is heavy. As such, liquidity tends to be a matter of “degree” (relative concept). Assets are often shown in a Balance Sheet either in ascending or descending order of liquidity.

At the one extreme, there is cash in hand (treated as 100 percent liquid). At the other extreme, there may be fictitious/intangible assets like goodwill (whose level of liquidity, according to commercial/conservative accounting practice, may be taken to be zero), between these two extremes fall most of the assets with their liquidity level above zero and below 100. However, some line of demarcation has to be drawn to distinguish the "liquid" from "illiquid" assets. On the basis of this classification, the ratio of liquid assets to the current liabilities of a business may be termed as "liquidity ratio" (also known, though somewhat erroneously, as "cash ratio"). The term liquidity ratio, in a different context, connotes the proportion of the total assets of a bank (say 37 percent) which are held in the form of cash and (other) liquid assets. For the purpose of credit control, a standard liquidity ratio (SLR), or a set of several ratios, may be prescribed by the central bank of a country (or such other regulatory agency),

Not one liquidity ratio, but several such ratios, may be worked out, particularly in the non-banking group of industries. In this context, certain "rules of thumb" have come into vogue, especially with regard to "current ratio" (2:1) and "quick ratio/acid test ratio" (1:1). The former is a ratio of current assets to current liabilities, whereas the latter is a ratio of quick (defensive) assets (inventories and prepaid expenses being subtracted from current assets) to current liabilities. Thus, both these ratios have the same denominator (current liabilities), whereas the numerator is usually different (unless there are no inventories/prepaid expenses). The rule of thumb suggests that current assets should-be twice the current liabilities, whereas quick assets should fully cover (be equal to) current liabilities. The idea is that there should be sufficient cushion so that, even if the current assets depreciate by 50 percent, the current liabilities can still be met in full.

However, expert studies in this field, like the one conducted by a Committee headed by Mr. P.L. Tandon (an outstanding management practitioner of India), go to suggest that such ratio norms cannot be deemed to be sacrosanct. Even the body temperature of every human being need not necessarily conform to the medical norm (98.4/98.6 F). Many individuals are quite normal and earthy with 97.5 F (on the lower side) or even with 99.0 F (on the higher side). This is true of liquidity ratios. A firm with a current ratio of 1.5:1 (low), or even with 2.5:1 (high), be quite sound financially. In fact, these ratios are bound to vary from industry to industry, from firm to firm, and even for the same firm from time to time. In real life situations, the range of variations may be much greater than what has been indicated above.

At this stage, it may be pertinent to perceive the dividing line between fixed and current assets. Functionally, fixed assets are acquired to be retained in an organization for being used again and again in the process of production (until they get worn out or obsolete, so as to be scrapped and/or sold). As against this, current assets (besides cash) are acquired for being processed/converted into cash at the earliest opportunity. As such, wood/steel/other inputs used to build a ship would constitute current assets even though the production turnover .cycle extends to two/three years. On the other hand, a farmer's plough would be a fixed asset, even if it is replaced twice within one year. However, for reasons of practical convenience, current assets are often defined to mean those items which are not likely to stay in an undertaking beyond one year. By implication, any item staying for a longer period may qualify to be categorized as a fixed asset.

It may now be relevant to spell out the distinction between current and quick assets. The main question is: What is the logic of treating receivables as quick assets, while inventories are excluded from that category? The distinction hinges both on commercial convention and legalistic interpretation. Once the goods are sold (or services rendered), the customers/ clients are obliged to clear their bills by the last date (or within days of grace) set for the purpose. Failure to do so may involve not only legal proceedings but also sudden erosion of goodwill in the business world. That is why even those businessmen, who commit defaults in the payment of taxes due to government/other public authorities, are quite punctilious in settling their acceptances (bills of exchange). On the other hand, even the inventories of finished stock cannot be thrust upon an unwilling customer (unless compulsory sale is envisaged under a legally enforceable agreement).

Moreover, in the normal course of business, there is no question of selling raw materials or goods-in-process (before their transformation into finished goods as interpreted in the particular context). Further, even when finished inventories are sold, they have yet to pass through the next stage (receivables) in the case of credit sales. Of course, there may be certain situations wherein, due to heavy pressure of demand, inventories of finished goods (which can attract ready/cash sales, or even advance payment) appear to be more liquid than receivables (specially, if these are aged ones). Advances to suppliers may represent a stage even farther from cash than inventories. The logic of excluding these and prepaid expenses (like unexpired insurance premium), from the category of quick assets, is that these are not likely to realize anything in cash. However, these items generally get included in current, assets under the "one year for rule" (since their usual stay is for less than twelve months). On this score, a reference to "interval ratios," discussed later in this chapter (3.4.25), may also be relevant.

Besides current ratio (first) and quick (acid test) ratio (second), a number of other liquidity ratios may be thought of.

Third, the relationship of net working capital (current assets minus current liabilities) with inventory (stock-in-trade) may be looked into. Presuming that the three main current assets are inventory, receivables and cash, whereas current liabilities are mainly represented by trade creditors (payables), the ratio of net working capital to inventory should be greater than unity. Its excess over "one" would be in margin of safety represented by cash and the excess of receivables (trade debtors over payables (trade creditors), inventory being a common factor both with the numerator and the denominator.

Fourth, the ratio of net working capital to receivables may be worked out. Assuming a near equality of receivables amount payable and a near zero level of cash, such a ratio would, in effect, measure the relationship between inventory (non-quick assets) and receivables (quick asset), the two main current assets. If the ratio is greater than unity, it would point toward the preponderance of the "non-quick" component over the "quick" component of current assets. If cash is considerable, a modified version of this ratio (non-quick current assets to quick assets) may be worked out. So also, the modified ratio may be more relevant to a situation in which credit sales (and, as such, receivables) are non-existent or insignificant.

Fifth, the ratio of short-term loans/bank borrowings to working capital gap may be worked out. If this ratio is unity (=1), it would go to indicate that the entire working capital gap (current assets minus trade creditors) has been financed by short-term loans, and that no part of it is a strain on the long-term fund of the firm (as represented by shares, debentures, etc.) Such ratio may be quite meaningful for the commercial bank also when a borrowing firm approaches it for loan. Likewise, when public deposits are being invited by a firm, the prospective depositors (at least the enlightened lot) can keep this ratio in view. A modified version of such a ratio may be the relationship between short-term loans (numerator) and net working capital (denominator). Assuming that the current ratio conforms to the rule-of-thumb (2:1), further modified nation would, in essence, reveal the relationship between short-term loans and other current liabilities (trade creditor). Assuming that a near equality between payables (trade creditors) and receivables (trade debtors), the modified version of the ratio would reflect the relationship between short-term loans and receivables.

Sixth, the ratio of short-term loans to gross working capital (current assets) may be computed. If this ratio is greater than unity (all extreme position), it would go to suggest that short-term loans are being used to finance non-current (fixed) assets. Such a state of dependence on commercial banks or short-term public deposits would be interpreted, in terms of conventional standards of prudence, as a sign of weakness. In case this ratio is 0.50 (50 percent) or more, but less than 1.00 (100 percent), it would still be a violation of the rule-of-thumb. That is, current ratio would fall below 2.00 (20 percent), more so after taking into account the trade creditors. Assuming a near-parity between trade creditors and other short-term liabilities, this ratio (of short-term funds to gross working capital) should not exceed 0.25 (25 percent) if the rule-of-thumb is to be honoured.

Seventh, the ratio of net working capital to all long-term funds may be worked out. Assuming a near parity between payables (trade creditors) and receivables (trade debtors), this ratio would measure, in essence, that part of long-term funds which is being maintained in the form of inventories and cash. As such, a high ratio may be indicative of overstocking or over optimum cash maintenance. Since, under ideal conditions of materials/financial management, one can think of "nil inventories" and "nil cash balance", the ratio of net working capital should be quite low. If this ratio is 0.10, it would go to suggest that long-term funds cover the net working capital burden ten times. So to say, the shock-absorbing apparatus of the firm is quite capable of containing seasonal upswings of demand on working capital.

Eighth, the ratio of net working capital to tangible assets may be computed. Assuming a near parity between payables (trade creditors) and receivables (trade debtors), this ratio would go to indicate the proportion of tangible assets held in the form of inventories and cash. Alternatively, with the same assumption, the ratio of current assets minus receivables to (total) tangible assets may be worked out. So to say, this is a ratio of the part to the whole. As such, it can never exceed unity. Ordinarily, it may be as low as 0.25 (25. percent). However, it may be higher for a commercial (trading) undertaking and lower for an industrial establishment (in particular, for heavy/capital intensive industries). Thus, the ratio throws some on the degree of capital intensity. Further, any abnormality in this ratio may also be a warning signal regarding sickness/impending failure. If the proportion of net working capital is too high; it may be the first warning to suggest that a firm is unable to 'utilize its liquid resources in an optimum fashion. And when this ratio is follow it may be the final account of the firm's inefficiency, the fixed assets might have to be sold to keep the firm going for some time more.

However, there may be seasonal/temporary ups and downs which are not, necessarily, any indication of failure. The term "tangible assets", according to dictionary meaning, are those which can be touched. In commercial parlance they imply concrete items, capable of realizing (being sold) independently. As such, fictitious/notional items like preliminary expenses, accumulated loss, and even goodwill may get excluded. If these are taken into account, the ratio of networking capital to total assets may be calculated.

Ninth, the ratio of current liabilities (short-term debt) to tangible assets may be-worked out. Normally, this ratio may be quite. low, say 0.20 (20 percent) or 0.25 (25 percent), indicating that current liabilities are covered five or four times by (total) tangible assets. This is a measure of liquidity over and above the current ratio which indicates this coverage by current assets only (twice, according to the rule-of-thumb). Assuming a near parity between current assets and non-current (tangible) assets, the ratio of current liabilities to tangible assets should be 0.25 (25 percent) in terms of the rule-of-thumb. Accordingly, if this ratio goes up to 0.50 (50 percent), or above, it might be a sign of an impending failure. At the other extra life if non-current (tangible) assets stand at a figure four times that of current assets, the norm of such a ratio would appear at 0.10 (10 percent) only according to the rule-of-thumb.

Tenth, the ratio of trade creditors to inventories may be worked out. Apparently an insignificant relationship, Professor V.S. Murty puts it at the top among liquidity ratios. Assuming a near-parity between trade creditors and trade debtors, and a near-zero cash balance, the norm of such a ratio might be unity (1:1) in terms of the rule-of-thumb. The possible-significance of this ratio lies in testing if trade creditors are-fully covered by inventories. Sometimes, the ratio of "short-term bank borrowings minus cash and bank balance" to "inventories plus-trade debtors" is worked out.

Eleventh, the ratio of current assets (or working capital) to fixed assets may be calculated. Like the other ten ratios referred to above, this also is a Balance Sheet Ratio. That is, both the numerator and denominator can be located within a Balance Sheet. However, although it throws light on the liquidity position of a firm, there is a school of thought which prefers to treat it as an activity ratio on the plea that the-denominator (gross operating fixed assets) has no liquidity component as such; it is a long-term basis of the level of business activity. It may, however, be mentioned that the ratio of current assets to fixed assets can be indicative of over-optimum or under-optimum liquidity only on the basis of varying norms for various industries/units (since a single norm to cover a wide canvas of activity is almost unthinkable). For example, if 0.25 (25 percent) is an established norm of this ratio for a capital intensive/heavy industry, an actual ratio of 0.20 (20 percent) would imply under-optimum liquidity, and an actual ratio of 0.30 (30 percent) would mean over-optimum liquidity.

Likewise, the norm for a labour intensive/medium industry may be (say) 0.40 (40 percent or 0.50 (50 percent), and that for light industry/trading activity it may be (say) 0.75 (75 percent) or even higher. Departures of actual ratios from norms, would, then throw light on the level of liquidity. A similar purpose may be achieved by calculating the ratio of current (or quick assets to total assets (instead of fixed assets only).

Twelfth, the ratio of cash to total assets may be worked out. This would go to indicate the extent to which the resources of a firm may be deemed to be liquid with 100 percent certainty. However, it may be kept in view that nothing; can be so certain in an uncertain world; for, commercial banks can fail, and even the cash in chest may become illiquid in the event of demonetization (or otherwise, too, if people lose confidence in paper currency or in coins with low intrinsic worth). Moreover, a large amount of cash in hand may mean more of physical hazard (like theft), as also moral hazard (like defalcation). Not only this, if the norm of nil (near-zero) cash balance is applied as a test of good financial management, a low ratio of cash to total assets may be a sign of strength, rather than that of weakness (poor liquidity or insolvency) as interpreted in a study of the failure of Dutch firms (1978). Here, CBT (point of time when anticipated cash balance would be less than zero) was the basis of "bankruptcy prediction model."

Further, the actual requirement of cash (and, so also the norm of its relationship to total assets) may vary from time to time (according to the prevailing environment), industry to industry and unit to unit. The "variability of liquidity" may be worked out on the basis of standard deviation/coefficient of variation, so that relevant norms can be inferred and kept in view. Thus, a ratio of 0.03 (3 percent) may appear to be on high side with a norm of 0.02 (2 percent), and on the low side if the norm is <0.05 (5 percent). A variant of this relationship may be the ratio of cash to tangible assets (instead of total assets). Alternatively, the ratio of cash to current liabilities may be computed.

Thirteenth, fourteenth and fifteenth may be the ratios of cash, receivables and inventories (respectively) to current assets (or current liabilities). If current assets are taken as the denominator, all these would 20 to depict the relationships of various parts (components) to the whole (current assets). That is, if current assets have only these three components, a summation of these ratios would be unity. For example, if the ratio of the cash to current assets is 0.10 (10 percent), and that of receivables to current assets is 0.30 (30 percent), the ratio of inventories to current assets would be 0.60 (60 percent). These ratios may be helpful in revealing the extent to which current assets are "quick". If the first two ratios (thirteenth and fourteenth) are added up, there would emerge another (sixteenth) relationship, viz. the ratio of quick assets to current, assets (0.40 or 40 percent in this case). According to the rule of thumb, it should not fall below 0.50 (50 percent). A variant of the sixteenth ratio may be the "ratio of quick assets to - total/tangible assets."

Seventeenth, the ratio of quick assets to inventories may be worked out. In terms of the rule of thumb, it should be less than unity (1:1). That is, if inventories are more than quick assets (cash plus receivables), while the current ratio (first) is normal (2:1), the quick ratio (second) is bound to fall below the norm (1:1). This is based on the assumption that current assets have only three components (cash, receivables and inventories). A falling ratio of quick assets to inventories may be an indication of a firm's inability to process inputs, or to sell finished goods (that is, to convert inventories into receivables/cash), sufficiently fast. To have more light in this regard, the ratio of quick assets to finished inventories may be worked out separately. For this purpose, the denominator may be decomposed (say) into raw materials, goods-in-process, and finished goods.

The list of seventeen ratios given above to measure liquidity is only indicative and not exhaustive. One can go on thinking of newer and newer relationships. Some writers (in particular, Marc Blum) have classified liquidity into (a) short-run liquidity, and (b) long-run liquidity (described as solvency or leverage by certain other writers). Ratios relating to the latter would be taken up later. Prior to the same, it is proposed to examine another dimension of liquidity through some of the "activity ratios" (relationship of sales/turnover with certain assets/liabilities). These may also be described as "turnover ratios" (implying the completion of an activity cycle, or a business process with sales of goods/services).

3.2 Activity/Turnover Ratios

The term activity (act/action) is of French/Latin origin. It is derived from "acts" (a doing)/"acetum" (thing done), past participle of "agree" (to do). For a business, sales represent the main plank of activity. As such, a number of relationships may be thought of. First, the ratio of turnover (cost of goods sold, or sales, during an accounting period) to inventories (average level of stock-in-trade obtaining during the accountant period, or the figure on the last day of that period) may be worked out. Since the inventories (denominator) are shown in the Balance Sheet usually at cost (unless, the market price is lower), the turnover (numerator) should also be expressed at cost to give precision to ratio analysis. With the same objective in view, inventories (denominator) should be stated at their average level and not at the level obtaining on the last day of an accounting period; for, the closing balance may not be truly representative, either due to accidental/seasonal situations, or due to design (window-dressing).

However, since it may be difficult to read the cost of goods sold from the Income Statement (Trading/Profit and Loss Account), and even more difficult to arrive at an average figure from the level of inventories as appearing on the assets side of a Balance Sheet, the turnover-inventories ratio is arrived at, very often in actual practice, on a rough-and-ready basis. The ratio is intended to give an idea of the amount of working capital locked up in inventories to attain a particular level of sales. It may vary with the nature of activity. For example, this ratio may be quite low (say unity or 1) for a shipbuilding unit, wherein (because of the long cycle of production and the slow movement of goods up to the final point of sales) investment in inventories may be turned over only once in an accounting year. In contrast to this, an ice-cream factory may have a very high turnover-inventories ratio (say 300); for (because of the very short process of manufacturing, and the highly perishable nature of goods), it may be able to turn over its investment in inventories almost every day (and, so, some three hundred times in an accounting year). The ratio may also vary on account of the varying levels of managerial efficiency (in buying, storing, processing, transporting, selling and other such activities). These variations can be read in the 'form of deviations from norms applicable to particular categories of industries/units. Thus, a ratio of 2 (two) may be deemed quite well for a shipbuilding unit, whereas a ratio of 150 may appear poor for an ice cream factory. To get more light on precise relationships, the turnover-inventories ratio may be decomposed into several descendant ratios, such as:

The ratio of turnover to raw materials in stock;

The ratio of turnover to goods-in-process; and

The ratio of turnover to finished goods in stock.

Second, the ratio of receivables (average level of accounts receivables/trade debtors during an accounting period, or the figure appearing in the Balance Sheet at the end of such period) to turnover (credit sales during the. accounting period) may be calculated. The figure appearing in respect of accounts receivable/trade debtors on the assets side of a Balance Sheet may be deemed reliable for this purpose (as numerator) if there are no major upswings/downswings in business, and (also) if there is no element of window-dressing as such. In any case, this is the usual practice on grounds of convenience; for the process of averaging out is complex and the collection of relevant information (normally not available in financial statements) may be difficult.

Sometimes, information is not available separately (at least in the Income Statement or Trading/Profit and Loss Account) regarding credit sales. In such a situation, the total turnover (comprising both credit and cash sales) is taken as the denominator. This introduces an element of inaccuracy which, of course, may be minor in case sales are few and far between. The ratio of receivables to turnover is also (and perhaps better) known as the "debtors' ratio" or "average collection period". It is expressed in a time dimension (ageing schedules may be looked into later under 3.2.15-18). Thus, if (average) receivables (trade debtors) amount to Rs. 24,000 and annual (credit) sales figure at Rs. 96,000, the quotient (debtors ratio) would be 0.25 (one-fourth) year. If it is intended to express this ratio in months, it may be multiplied by 12, so that the ratio would be three months. When multiplied by 52, the debtors' ratio would appear as 13 weeks. In case it is multiplied by 365 (or 366) the same would be expressed as 91 days (or so).

That is, in this particular case, when goods are sold on credit, the (average) expectation is that the receivables would realize after-one fourth year, three months, thirteen weeks, or ninety-one days (average collection period). If, for the same level of (credit) sales, (average) receivables go up to Rs. 32,000, the average collection period (debtors' ratio) would rise to one-third year, four months, 17.3 weeks, or 122 days (approximately). This, in effect, would mean a worsening of the terms of trade resulting in increased demand of working capital for the same level of business. That is the firm's (short-term) resources are being locked1 up with the trade debtors for a longer duration (on an average). It can also be interpreted as a diminution in the goodwill of the firm, or as a deliberate attempt to thrust goods (sales) on an unwilling market (customers). After looking into (comparable) debtors' ratios of competing firms, the change may appear as a symptom of general recession in the industry as a whole, or as an indication of that particular firms' impending failure. A variant of this relationship may be the ratio of (credit) "sales, to (average) receivables (that is, the denominator becomes the numerator and vice versa) to show how many times the receivables (trade debtors) are turned over in an accounting period. If debtors ratio is 0.25 (one-fourth year), the turnover ratio (reciprocal) would be 4 (four).

Third, the ratio of payables (average level of accounts payable/trade creditors during an accounting period, of the figure appearing in the Balance Sheet at the end of such period to credit purchases (during the accounting period) may be. worked out. The quotient is known as the "creditor's ratio" or "average payment period." It is the counterpart of "debtor's ratio" or "average collection period," as discussed in the earlier paragraph. The sources of error here, too, may be similar, such as the non-availability of separate figures in respect of credit purchases (leading to the use of total, purchases as the denominator), the non-representative character of the figure of trade creditors as appearing in the Balance Sheet, and the no availability of the average figure in respect thereof (the numerator). The computation process is also similar.

Thus, if (average) payables (trade creditors) amount to Rs. 15,000 and annual (credit) purchases figure at Rs. 90,000, the creditors ratio (average payment period) would be 0.16 (one-sixth year), two months, 8.7 weeks, or 61 days (approximately). If, for the same level of (credit) purchases, (average) payables go up to Rs. 18,000, the average payment period (creditors ratio) would rise to 0.20 (one-fifth year), 2.4 months, 30.4 weeks, or 73 days. Such a change would signify an improvement in the terms of trade resulting in reduced demand of (net) working capital for the same level of activity. That is, the particular line is able to use, for a longer duration (in the latter situation), the resources belonging to other firms (which are selling goods to this firm of credit). Such a change may, normally, be indicative of better financial management. In fact, in order to have a fuller view of the picture, the creditor's ratio should be placed in juxtaposition powerful bearing on the volume/rapidity of turnover. This ratio is a pointer toward the maximum/optimum level of activity (sales) which can be generated with a given base of current assets (deemed to be of immediate relevance for generating/augmenting such activity).

Thus, if the sales of a firm rise from Rs. 60,000 to Rs. 80,000, while the current assets go up from Rs. 20,000 to Rs. 25,000, the ratio of turnover to gross working capital has improved from 3.0 to 3.2. Such an improvement may also manifest itself when the current assets remain constant while the sales go up, or when the sales remain constant while the current assets go down. Reverse situations (like relative decline in turnover or relative increase in gross working capital) may be indicative of deterioration in such ratio.

Fifth, the ratio of turnover (sales) to net working capital (current assets minus current liabilities) may be computed. Here, the numerator is the same as taken in the previous (fourth) ratio; out the denominator is net working capital instead of gross working capital. That is, current liabilities are subtracted from the earlier denominator. Sometimes, it is simplified to represent inventories plus receivables (trade debtors) minus payable (trade creditors). So to say, these three Balance Sheet items (two on the assets side, and one on the liabilities side) are presumed to have a powerful and an immediate bearing on sales turnover. The ratio of such turnover to net working capital seeks to measure the capacity of a firm to, generate/augment activity with the fund actually locked up in the form of short-term resources "as the base for such activity. To focus further attention on this aspect of the matter, ratios of "sales to cash" and "sales to quick assets" may be calculated.

Sixth, ratio of turnover (sales) to fixed assets (usually the net or depreciated value) may be worked out. Sometimes, the denominator is represented by gross operating fixed assets. That is, the non-operating fixed assets (having no significant/immediate bearing on sales turnover) are excluded from reckoning, and the relevant fixed assets are shown at their gross value (before deducting depreciation). For example, a firm may have bought land (possibly at exorbitant price in an era of inflation) with the intention of constructing head office buildings. Until the land is actually utilized for the purpose, (and the head office starts functioning at that place), it is clearly a non-operating fixed asset having hardly any relationship with the sales turnover activity. Even after the head office buildings have been constructed (and put into use for administrative purposes), their relationship with the volume of sales may not be as intimate as in the case of plant/machinery and factory premises (or farm land in case of agriculture/agro-based industries).

The logic behind putting gross fixed assets as the denominator is to steer clear of varying depreciation policies followed by different firms, or even by the same firm at different points of time conditioned by the changing whims of top management, price behaviour, taxation laws (of several countries relevant to multinational business) and other dimensions of change. In fact, particularly in an era of inflation, a firm may have built up a depreciation fund (appearing on the liabilities side of its Balance Sheet) far in excess of the gross value (original/historical cost appearing on the assets side of its Balance Sheet) of the relevant fixed asset(s). In such a situation, the net/depreciated value would be negative, and the ratio of turnover to fixed assets would become indeterminate. However, ignoring the element of depreciation may not necessarily be a panacea for all the ills associated with this ratio.

The market value (replacement cost at current/anticipated price level) of certain fixed assets may be far in excess of their gross value (original/historical cost) due to far-reaching depreciation in the internal/external value of a currency (caused by serious inflation or devaluation). Would, then, gross fixed assets be up valued, for computing the ratio, so that the same could be in line with such competing firms as might have acquired comparable assets at a much higher price? Or, the real value of' certain fixed assets may have actually depreciated to a near-zero level (as in the case of an exhausted mine or oil well) so that, in spite of price inflation, the use of gross fixed assets as a denominator may be most an absurdity. The element of inflation does not always compensate appropriately for the element of depreciation. In fact, it may not even be logical to mix up these two elements while working out an activity ratio. Of course, there is some force in the argument that, since the numerator (turnover) is expressed in terms of current price level, the denominator (fixed assets) may also be written accordingly.

However, the practical feasibility of such a proposition is rather limited on account of the Arbitrary elements entering the revaluation of (partly used up) fixed assets, more so if these are in the form of such makes of machines which are no longer manufactured/imported/quoted in the market. Further, unless a comprehensive system of indexation (revaluation or inflation accounting) is in vogue, it may be difficult to apply this concept to some fixed assets only. It may also call for a two-column approach on both sides of the Balance Sheet indicating historical and current values (respectively) of various items, along with emerging suspense accounts and other complications.

Seventh, the ratio of turnover (sales) to total assets may be computed. Here the numerator is the same as in the previous (sixth) ratio. But the denominator has a wider coverage (total assets instead of fixed assets only). It seeks to combine the base of the sixth ratio (fixed assets) with that of the fourth ratio (current assets). Presuming that these are the only two constituents of "total assets," the ratio of turnover to total assets (seventh ratio) would be the reciprocal of the "summation of the reciprocals of fourth and sixth ratios." However, this would not be so if a Balance Sheet contains certain assets which fall neither in the category of fixed assets nor in that of current assets.

Moreover, valuation problems relating to the denominator may get quite complicated in view of the diverse considerations governing fixed, current and other assets like goodwill and patents, whose values, as appearing in a Balance Sheet, may be highly discretionary/arbitrary. Further, fictitious assets like accumulated loss may have no relationship, as such, with the sales turnover. Therefore, a firm may like to work out a variant of the relationship as represented by the ratio of turnover (sales) to tangible assets (instead of total assets). Alternatively, net worth (tangible assets minus outside liabilities) may be taken as the denominator. Another variant may take "sales (net of excise)" as the numerator, in case the element of indirect taxation is substantial and highly variable. Yet another variant may have "average tangible assets" as the denominator, if it is found that the Balance Sheet figures are not sufficiently representative, on account of constant/violent fluctuations in the level of such assets during the course of an accounting period, A simple/crude method of averaging, often adopted in practice, is to divide the summation of opening and closing figures by two.

Eighth, the ratio of turnover (sales) to "the excess-of receivables over payables (trade debtors minus trade creditors)" may be worked out. Such a ratio is based on the implicit assumption that (average) trade debtors are always greater than (average) trade creditors; for, if this is not so, the ratio becomes indeterminate. The said assumption stems from the basic philosophy that a business is run for profit (or that, in any case, it must break even and avoid loss). As such, the cost of goods (input) purchased would, normally, be lower than the price of goods (output) sold. Presuming that all the purchases and sales are on credit, the amount of payables would be less than that of receivables. Even then, there could appear exceptional situations when a big chunk of bad debts pull down the latter below the level of the former. However, having a normal situation in view, the ratio of sales to "trade debtors minus trade creditors" would be a function of four vital variables:

Extent of processing;

Gross margin of profit;

Average payment period; and

Average collection period.

In case there is parity between the last two variables, these can be merged into a single consideration. If there is a purely trading activity, the first consideration would disappear. As such, gross margin and average period of credit (either way) would be the two considerations relevant to the ratio. Thus, if gross margin is 50 percent on sales and the average period of credit is 73 days, the ratio of sales to "trade debtors minus trade creditors" would be 10, worked out as follows:

Selling price x number of days in the accounting period
Gross margin x average period of credit in days

$$= \frac{100}{50} \times \frac{365}{73}$$

$$= 2 \times 5 = 10$$

Ninth, a "super ratio" of average payment period (creditor's ratio) to average collection period (debtor's ratio) may be worked out. A new name may be given to it, such as "terms of trade ratio" or "terms of credit ratio." At this stage, it may be convenient to revert to the type situations visualized under second and third activity ratios (debtor's ratio and creditor's ratio) discussed earlier. In the first situation, the average payment period was 61, whereas the average collection period was figured at 91 (in days). So the terms of trade ratio would be 0.67 (61 divided by 91). This quotient may be multiplied by 100 if the intention is to express this ratio as a percentage index (67 percent; in the second situation, the average payment period was 73, while the average collection period stood at 122. As such, the terms of trade ratio would be 0.60 (or 60 percent). Thus, in both the situations, the ratio was below unity (<l) or below 100 percent. As such, the terms of trade were unfavourable to the firm which experienced further deterioration in the second situation. That is, this firm had to yield more in extending credit to other firms than what other firms had to yield in accommodating this particular firm.

Tenth, the ratio of "receivables (trade debtors) plus

advances to suppliers" to turnover (sales) may be calculated. This may be a useful supplement to the second ratio (average collection period), in case substantial amounts have been advanced to suppliers for procuring certain highly essential/scarce inputs. In a sense, this is indicative of extreme deterioration in the terms of trade, so that, far from being able to avail the facility of buying goods on credit, the firm has to pay (a substantial part of the price) in advance. Thus, the firm has to lock up a greater part of its fund in the form of working capital (over and above what normally gets locked up in the form of trade debtors) as represented by advances to suppliers. To overcome this disadvantage, the firm may be called upon to push up its sales turnover. In some cases, "advances to suppliers" may be in respect of capital equipment (such as aircraft for an airline) which is of a "made-to-order" or "proprietary" character. If so, this item would represent a replica of the fixed assets to be acquired after some time (say, two or three years).

Eleventh, the ratio of turnover (cost of goods sold, or sales net of excise, during an accounting period) to "invent rise plus advances to supplies" may be worked out. This m be a useful supplement to the first ratio (relationship between turnover and inventories), so that advances to suppliers (which can be termed as "embryonic inventories") can also be take into account. Both additional inventories and advances suppliers have an identical impact with regard to (augmented working capital requirements. The difference lies in respect storage cost which is a burden in respect of actual inventor (but not so with embryonic inventories).

Twelfth, the ratio of payables (trade creditors) turnover (sales, or cost of goods sold, during an accounting period) may be computed. Presuming that all the purchases is made on credit, and that there is a given "average payment period (creditors ratio)", this ratio would in effect, measure the relationship between purchases and sales. The variability such a relationship would then be a function of the gross ratio on sales ("mark up" of the selling price above the cost price the efficiency with which input(s) can be transformed into output(s) and the speed with which output(s) can take the for of sales (so as to establish some correspondence between initial and ultimate sales). In view of the time lag involve in the process, the figure of trade creditors appearing in Balance Sheet, on the last day of the accounting period, m not be an appropriate numerator. It may be preferable to leverage figure, or the figure appearing at the mid-point the accounting year. If the time lag is long enough, even the opening balance (trade creditors appearing in the Balance Sheet at the end of the previous accounting year) may serve as suitable numerator.

Thirteenth, the ratio of current liabilities (the creditors and other current liabilities) to turnover (cost of goods sold or sales net of excise) may be calculated. Here, the coverage of the numerator is wider than that indicated in the earlier ratio, so that not only trade creditors, but also to the current liabilities like outstanding expenses/dues are taken in account. Thus, even though current liabilities reduce to requirement of net working capital, as also the pressure on firm's fund, the sales activity must be adequate enough justify a particular level of current liabilities. If this is not so, it may not be possible for the firm to collect enough cash in course of time, for their timely repayment. As such, (what normally constitutes), a favourable creditors ratio might turn into a burden, leading the firm toward insolvency.

Fourteenth, the ratio of turnover (sales) to capital employed (the capital in use in a business) may be worked out. According to the Penguin Dictionary of Economics (1980), "there is no universally agreed definition of the term. It is sometimes taken to mean net assets (i.e. fixed plus current assets minus current liabilities), but more usually bank loans and overdrafts are included and other adjustments made for the purpose of calculating the return on net capital employed (rate of return), such as the exclusion of intangible assets and the revaluation of trade investments at market prices." Thus, if current liabilities are not excluded, and certain other adjustments are not made, the term "capital employed", as denominator, would mean the same as "total assets". As such, this would be a repetition of the seventh ratio. Even if intangible assets are excluded, it would be a variant of the seventh ratio; as already indicated along with the same (ratio of sales to tangible assets). It may as well mean an integration of the fourth ratio (ratio of sales to gross working capital or current assets) with the sixth ratio (ratio of sales to fixed assets). In case current liabilities are excluded (from the denominator), the resultant ratio can be represented as an integration of the sixth ratio with the fifth ratio (ratio of sales to net working capital). Another way of arriving at the denominator may be to add non-current liabilities to owners' equity. If there are no adjustments as such, one may arrive at the same destination through this approach which, of course, may be more appropriate for ratios based on net worth, and designed to measure the strength of equity.

The aforesaid coverage of fourteen activity ratios is only indicative and not exhaustive. In particular, it does not cover the relationships falling outside the customary periphery of financial management. The activity ratios discussed above have a perceptible bearing on liquidity also. Before passing on to other categories of financial ratios, it may be relevant to dwell on the ratios emanating from "ageing schedules" which provide vital information in respect of liquidity (even though these relationships may be rather remote in the context of activity ratios) (Table 3.1).

These schedules (ratios/percentages) may reveal the inner (qualitative) dimensions of the second ratio (average collection period), the third ratio (average payment period), and the ninth ratio (a super ratio of debtors and creditors ratio). If the two situations discussed earlier under the second ratio (debtor's ratio) are stretched further, the following table can be constructed to throw light on the inner (qualitative) dimensions of receivables (trade debtors) on the basis of ageing schedules:

Table 3.1: Ageing Schedules of Receivables

Period (days)	Situation I Amount (Rs.) Percentage		Situation 11 Amount (Rs.) Percentage	
1- 30	2,400	10	9,600	30
31- 60	3,600	15	8,000	25
61- 90	4,800	20	6,400	20
91-120	-6,000	25	4,800	15
Over 1 0	7,200	30	3,2*00	10
Total	24,000	100	32,000	100

The amount of (credit) sales, in both the situations (as indicated earlier), was Rs. 96,000. If the ageing schedules are not constructed, the average collection period (debtors ratio) would appear to have gone up from 91 days to 122 days (quite an unfavourable trend both in terms of liquidity and activity ratios). However, when weighted averages are worked out on the basis of ageing schedules (within an assumption that the mid-point of last class interval is 150 days), the average collection period would appear to have gone down from 95 days to 62 days (quite a favourable trend both in terms of liquidity and activity ratios). It is significant to note that, in the first situation, the weighted average (95) is not very different from (only slightly higher than) the ordinary average (91 days). But, in the second situation, the weighted average (62) is very much lower than (only about half of) the ordinary average (122).

The tables have been turned on account of a radical change (of a favourable character) in the ageing composition of trade debtors. The earlier situation was grave inasmuch as 55 percent of receivables were outstanding for more than 90 days, the proportion of such "old" (overdue) receivables having gone down now to as low as 25 percent (from Rs. 13,200 to Rs. 8,000 in amount). On the other hand, the proportion of "young" receivables (within 60 days) has gone up from 25 percent to 55 percent (from Rs. 6,000 to Rs. 17,600 in amount). In the "middle-age,' group (61-90 days) the proportion has remained constant (20 percent), though the amount has varied from Rs. 4,800 to Rs. 6,400 (in the context of a bigger base). Thus, in spite of a sizable (25 percent) increase in the total amount of trade debtors, the firm finds itself in a more comfortable position in the second situation. Ageing schedules can be prepared in respect of payables (trade creditors) also, even though the usual focus in this regard is on receivables (Table 3.2). If the two situations discussed earlier in connection with the third ratio (creditors ratio) are stretched further, the following table can be constructed to throw light on the inner (qualitative) dimensions of payables (trade creditors) on the basis of ageing schedules:

Table 3.2: Ageing Schedules of Payables

Period	**Situation I**		**Situation If**	
(days)	**Amount (Rs)**	**Percentage**	**Amount (Rs)**	**Percentag**
1-30	1,500	10	7,200	40
31-60	3,00.0	20	5,400	30
61-90	4,500	30	3,600	20
Over 90	6,000	40	1,800	10
Total	15,000	100	18,000	100

The amount of (credit) purchases, in both the positions (as indicated earlier), was Rs. 90,000. If the age schedules are not constructed, the average payment period (creditor's ratio) would appear to have gone up from 61 day 73 days (an apparently favourable trend supposed to reduce pressure on the requirement of net working capital for sustaining the same level of activity). However, when weighted averages are worked out on the basis of ageing schedules (an assumption that the mid-point of the last class interval 120), the average payment period would appear to have gone down from 81 days to 47 days (quite an unfavourable trade in terms of liquidity and activity ratio). This qualitative deterioration is typified by the fact that 70 percent of the trade credit now (as against 30 percent previously) belong to the young group (not exceeding 60 days). Further, the middle-age group (61-90 days) now encompasses only 20 percent (as age 30 percent previously); while the old-age group (over 90 days) is left with just 10 percent (as against 40 percent previously) of the trade creditors. Putting the ageing schedules of receivables and payables in juxtaposition, Table 3.3 can be constructed to reveal the qualitative dimensions of difference between the two situations as visualized.

Table 3.3: Ageing Schedules of Receivables and Payables

		Situation I		**Situation II**	
	Age	**Receivables Percent**	**Payables Percent**	**Receivables Percent**	**Pay Percent**
1	Young (1-60 days)	25	30	55	70
2	Middle (61-90 days)	20	30	20	.. 20
3.	Old (Over 90 days)	55	40	25	10
4	Total	100	100	100	100

Looking at these percentages, it would appear that, in the young-age group, payables had greater concentration than receivables in both the situations; and, the "relative concentration" of payables has increased still further. In the middle-age group the relative concentration of payables, appearing in the first situation, was transformed into a position of priority in the second situation. In the old age group, receivables had greater concentration than payables in both the situations; and, the relative concentration of receivables has increased still further. A similar exercise can be gone through to compare the actual amounts (instead of percentages) of receivables and payables in the three age groups separately. Thus, in the young-age group, receivables rose from Rs. 6,000 to Rs. 17,600 (while payables rose at a marginally lower speed from Rs. 4,500 to Rs. 12,600). In the middle-age group, receivables rose from Rs. 4,800 to Rs. 6,400 (while payables fell from Rs. 4,500 to Rs. 3,600). The old-age group saw receivables fall from Rs. 13,200 to Rs. 8,000 (while payables fell much faster from Rs. 6,000 to Rs. 1,800).

Thus, the ratio of payables and receivables in the young-age group works out to 0.75 (Rs. 4,500 divided by Rs. 6,000) in the first situation and 0.72 (Rs. 12,600 divided by Rs. 17,600) in the second situation. In the middle-age group, this ratio fell steeply from 0.94 (Rs. 4,500 divided by Rs. 1,800) to 0.56 (Rs. 3,600 divided by Rs. 6,400). The old-age group saw a precipitate fall in the ratio from 0.45 (Rs. 6,000 divided by Rs. 13,200) to 0.22 or 0.23 (Rs. 1,800 divided by Rs. 8,000). The overall ratio of payables to receivables fell from 0.62 or 0.63 (Rs. 15,000 divided by Rs. 24,000) to 0.56 (Rs. 18,000 divided by Rs. 32,000).

On the basis of weighted averages emerging from ageing schedules of receivables and payables, the "super ratio" (terms of trade ratio) of average payment period (creditor's ratio) to average' collection period (debtor's ratio) would appear to have declined from 0.85 (81 divided by 95) to 0.76 (47 divided by 62). In the absence of ageing schedules, the terms of trade had been worked out (under ninth ratio) at 0.67 and 0.60 for the two situations (first and second) respectively. The magnitude of deterioration in the terms of trade, as revealed by these two sets of computations, is about the same. But the preparation of ageing schedules in respect of receivables and payables has served to indicate that the general level of these terms of trade in relation to unity is not so bad as revealed earlier. As fine tools for deeper probe, the following three sets of ratios may be added to the list of fourteen activity ratios discussed earlier:

Ageing ratios of receivables (fifteenth);

Ageing ratios of payables (sixteenth); and

Ageing ratios (super ratios) of payables and receivables (seventeenth).

3.3 Solvency/Leverage Ratios

The term solvency has had its origin in French "solver" and Latin "solver," implying capacity/ability to loosen, dissolve, explain, clear up, remove, find a satisfactory answer, and "pay all one's debts" (as used in commercial parlance). These debts, obviously, include both long-term and short-term obligations. However, the main focus is on the former, as against liquidity ratios which have the latter as their main plank. In fact, solvency is sometimes termed as "long-run liquidity". The term leverage, too, is of French ("levier"/"lever") and Latin ('levare') origin, implying the mechanical power/advantage gained by the use of a lever/handle/menas to an end (increased means of accomplishing some purpose). In commercial parlance, it implies the choice (manipulation) of an appropriate "capita" structure" which can ensure best/optimum return to the suppliers of capital. As viewed from the standpoint of owners/ equity shareholder's, it may stand for the possibility to maximizing the rate of dividend.

When looked at from the viewpoint of (long-term) creditors (holders of debentures/bonds)/preference shareholders, leverage may imply "coverage"' of fixed annual obligations (interest/preferential dividend) by the level of earnings, as also the prospect of repayment/redemption (as evident from the coverage of debt by owners' fund). Terms like "capital gearing" and "debt ratio" are in the same line, while the term "leverage" has been used widely in the United States. In the MDA Model developed by Altman (1968), distinction was sought to be established between leverage (Xs) and solvency while choosing the following five key ratios to represent five standard categories *(Journal of Finance,*

September 1968):

X_1=Liquidity (Ratio of Working Capital to Total Assets);

X_2=(Cumulative) Profitability (Ratio of Retained Earnings to Total Assets);

X_3=Leverage (Ratio of Earnings Before Interest and Taxes to Total Assets);

X_4=Solvency (Ratio of Market Value of Equity to Book Value of Total Debt); and

X_5=Activity (Ratio of Sales to Total Assets).

Altaian (E.I.), Haldeman (Robert G.), and Narayanan (P.) presented a revised and enlarged model in their paper entitled "Zeta Analysis: A New Model to Identify Bankruptcy Risk of Corporations" *(Journal of Banking and Finance,* Spring 1977). The seven key variables explaining corporate failure were represented as follows (to arrive at Z or "Zeta-score"):

X_1= Return on Assets (Ratio of Earnings before Interest and Taxes to Total Assets);

X_2= Stability of Earnings (Normalization Measure of Standard Error of estimates around a ten-year trend);

X_3= Debt Service (Ratio of Earnings before Interest and Taxes to Total Interest Payment);

X_4= Cumulative Profitability (Ratio of Retained Earnings to Total Assets);

X_5= Liquidity (Ratio of Current Assets to Current Liabilities);

X_6= Capitalization (Ratio of Equity to Total Capital); and

X_7= Size (Measured by Total Assets).

About the same time, Richard 'Tamer and Howard Tisshaw developed a 'Z Model' in their paper entitled "Going, Going, Gone-Four Factors which Predict Failure" *(Accountancy,* March 1977). This solvency model was based on four ratios only: profit before tax/current liabilities *(R1)*; current assets/total liabilities *(R_2);* current liabilities/total assets *(R_3);* and no credit interval *(R4),* examined later (3.4.25). With C_0 as a constant, tlle risk profile was measured by Z-score (discriminant score) as follows (Q. . . C_4 being ratio weights or coefficients).

Altman's leverage ratio (earlier X_3) verged on (current) profitability, and it ignored the extent to which a firm's resources might be represented by owners' fund (as against borrowings). As such, it overlooked the basic function of a lever (that is, "to raise" a bar at one end, by pressing it at another point, with a view to lifting/sustaining weight). So to say, leverage had not been visualized as any sliding ratio which might be adjusted on the basis of criticality or optimality. This was taken care of in the revised model. Here, it is proposed to take up a discussion of solvency and leverage ratios (as also capital structure/gearing/ debt/coverage ratios) under one umbrella.

First, the ratio of debt to equity (total debt or outside liabilities to net worth) may be worked out. The numerator by implication, would include not only long-term debt but also short-term debt (current liabilities). Preference share capital (particularly, if it is redeemable) may also be included therein. The denominator would be represented by equity share capital (ordinary and/or deferred shares, where permitted by law). Free reserves (available to equity shareholders/owners) may also form part of the denominator which may, then, be described as "net worth" (owner's/proprietor's fund/ shareholder's interest). Retained profits (general reserve) and realised capital gains (capital reserve) constitute the ostensible part of free reserves; but, if certain secret reserves are discernible (like those resulting from overstatement of liabilities or understatement of assets, say due to excessive depreciation/provision for bad debts), these also should be taken into account.

By the same token, free reserves would stand reduced if there has been understatement of liabilities or overstatement of assets. Preference share capital, if deemed to be part of net worth, has to be excluded from the numerator. But this may be done only when the preference shareholders are, in substance, the owners of a company (i.e. vested with decision-making power and the right to get participating! dividend beyond the fixed minimum). In India, preference shares, ordinarily, do not have voting rights unless their dividend is in arrear. These were made almost analogous to debenture holders under the Companies Act of 1956. Apart from this method of arriving at net worth (owners' capital *plus* free reserves), there is the alternative method of starting with total (tangible) assets and subtracting all third-party claims/ external liabilities *(excluding* equity capital, but *including* preference share capital if that is deemed analogous to debt).

As such, net worth is sometimes defined as "total assets *minus* long-term debt, minority interest, future tax and current liabilities" (with the implicit assumption that all the assets are tangible/realisable at their book values, and that all the liabilities are correctly stated in the Balance Sheet). Thus stated, the ratio of debt to net worth goes to indicate "how thick the owners' cushion is" for the protection of creditors in the event of financial erosion. For example, with debt standing at Rs. 40,000 and net worth being worked out at Rs. 80,000, the relevant ratio would be 1:2 or 0.50 (50 percent). Although there is no rule-of-thumb, a ratio of less than unity (<1) may be interpreted to mean that the capital structure is "low geared". A ratio of 1.1 (unity, or 1) may be indicative of a "medium geared" structure, which was adopted as the norm by the Government of India for many of their public enterprises in the era of planning initiated in 1951.

When the ratio is greater than unity (>1), it may be a pointer toward a "high geared" capital structure. It may, however, be mentioned that 'the usual denominator for working out gearing ratios is equity share capital and not net worth as such. Likewise, the usual numerator, for the purpose of capital gearing, is long-term debt (mainly debentures/bonds) and not total debt (all the creditors) as such. Moreover, it may, sometimes, be more relevant to work out the ratio of net worth (equity) to debt (long-term debt), so that the numerator takes the place of the denominator *and vice versa.* This latter ratio

(2.1), that is 2.0 (or 200 percent), would be a reciprocal of the former ratio (1:2), which is 0.50 (or 50 percent), as indicated in the above-mentioned example. The reciprocal (2.0) indicates explicit that debt is covered twice by equity which, as a cushion, is thick enough.

This can also be called as "coverage ratio" with its focus on solvency and equity/net worth being visualized is a security for the repayment of (long-term) debt. Another coverage ratio, with its focus on (what in certain quarters has been described as) leverage (relationship between earning power and interest on debt) would be examined later. A variant of "debt-equity ratio" may be "equity-total capital ratio".

Second, the ratio of long-term debt to net worth/equity (as inferred in the latter part of last paragraph) may be' calculated. This differs from the first ratio (as indicated in the earlier part of last paragraph) in that the numerator (or "the denominator in the case of "reciprocal" ratio) does not include short-term debt/current liabilities. The rationale for excluding trade creditors (and such other liabilities) emerges from the assumption that the liquidity ratios are good enough to take care of these items which are of a transitory and highly fluctuating character with no interest obligations as such. However, there is also another side of the coin, A good part of trade credit (emerging from non-cash purchases), as also commercial credit (bank loans), is, in essence, of a permanent character.

Thus, if the current liabilities of a firm range between Rs. 50,000 and Rs. 75,000 at different points of time, it virtually implies that a sum of Rs. 50,000 is a long-term debt (even though in disguise). This is the ellective position, in spite of frequent changes in the names of creditors, formal repayment of old loans, and entries in respect of new loans. Moreover, short-term obligations may, sometimes, be more pressing, so that an inability to meet the same (punctually) could mean an immediate invitation to insolvency. A commercial bank which commits a default in meeting its demand liabilities (or whose statutory liquidity ratio falls below the prescribed minimum) may have to close its doors instantaneously. Even in other lines of activity, a party which fails to honour its short-term acceptances (hands, bills of exchange, promissory notes, at the appointed time or within the stipulated period (including days of grace, if any), is likely to be treated as an "outcast" in the business world.

This, possibly, is much greater a risk (damage to goodwill) than what may be involved when there is a default in paying the amounts due to long-term lending in situations (such as IFCI and IDBI in India) on account of periodical interest/repayment of loans. Further, trade creditors/other current liabilities, too, may have an implicit (or even explicit) cost by way of interest. Thus, a firm may have to pay a higher price for goods purchased on credit, and it may also lose cash discount (or be called upon to pay penalty) on account of its failure to make timely payment in respect of short-term obligations (which may also lead to disconnection or withdrawal of basic facilities such as telephone/water/electricity).

Third, the ratio of long-term debt to permanent capital (equity plus non-current liabilities) may be computed. This, in fact, is the relationship between a part (long-term debt) and its whole (long-term debt *plus* owners' capital). Here, the numerator is the same as in the second ratio; but, the denominator is extended to cover the numerator also (beyond what is covered under the second, ratio). As such, this (third ratio) cannot exceed unity (1) unless owners' capital/equity is a negative figure (on account of accumulated loss, excessive drawings, or payment of dividend out of capital in excess of what is warranted by the level of profits). It may be added that a negative figure of owners' capital/equity would render the second ratio indeterminate; but, the third ratio can still be worked out (so long as the amount of long-term debt is greater than that negative figure).

Where permanent capital, as such, is nil or negative, even the third ratio would be indeterminate. But it may be rare for a going concern of sound standing to go on operating merely on the basis of the indirect finance provided by trade creditors/ other current liabilities. Such a situation could, no doubt, be a prelude to insolvency. The third ratio (as also the second ratio) would not be relevant at all to those firms which do not have any long-term debt. It may, of bourse, be a question of interpretation if public deposits (a very important source of .additional finance for many private sector and public sector undertakings) are to be treated as long-term debt. Since such deposits are not, normally, accepted for less than one year, these are not, as such, of a short-term character. However, as their formal term, usually, does n6t go beyond three or five years, these deposits are not so long-term either. One could, perhaps, describe these as medium-term funds. But even this description may not be meaningful if depositors can within their capital at short notice (say, three months), even though after a stipulated period (say, one year).

Of course, in actual practice, it may be extremely difficult for a depositor to wit draw his investment even after the expiry of the (full stipulated term. Some companies, particularly those in financial difficult may not respond to letters received from depositors, or add other dilatory tactics (to postpone the evil day), taking advantage of the fact that most depositors (specially, those of relative small means) cannot afford to go to law courts. In fact the judicial process may be even more time-consuming. As such public deposits could pass as long-term debt. So long as the general investment climate is congenial, and the relevant firm' goodwill is high, many depositors may (themselves) prefer to prolong (rather than cut short) the duration of their investment. But the situation may be very different in the event of a scare As such it may not be quite safe for companies to use public deposits as fixed capital. And if such deposits are employed by way of working capital only, it may, functionally, be inappropriate to treat the same as long-term debt. The ratio of long-term debt to permanent capital, which a borrowing company is able to maintain, may be a relevant criterion for scrutinizing loan applications received by long-term lending institutions. Even those intending to make public deposits may find it advantageous to examine such ratios of the companies concerned. If the relevant ratio is 0.50 (50 percent), or less, it might be a reasonably safe position for the lender who must, or course, examine both *ex-ante* (before lending) and *ex-post facto* (after taking into account the amount of loan/deposits) ratios.

Fourth, the ratio of long-term debt to total liabilities (or total assets, which would mean the same) may be calculated. Such a ratio measures the relationship between a part and the whole. As such, it can never go beyond unity. In actual practice, it may be much less, say 0.50 (50 percent), even for a company having high geared capital structure. For a low geared company, it may be less than 0.25 (25 percent). A variant of this relationship may be the ratio of long-term debt to tangible assets only.

Fifth, the ratio of (total) debt to tangible assets may be worked out. Here the denominator excludes fictitious/ intangible assets like accumulated loss, preliminary expenses, goodwill, patents, copyrights and trade marks. The numerator covers both current and long-term liabilities (which may include preference share capital also specially, when it is of a redeemable character). So computed, this ratio provides a specific measure of a firm's solvency. If the ratio is greater than unity (>1), there is a presumption of insolvency, inasmuch as the firm may not be in a position to repay all the debt even if the tangible assets are able to realize their full book value. When the ratio is unity (=1), the firm may drift toward insolvency even if there is a slight depreciation in the value of tangible assets. The ratio has to be *substantially* less than unity (<1) in order that a firm appears to be fairly solvent. A variant of this relationship may be the ratio of total debt to total assets.

Sixth, the ratio of fixed assets (net block) to net worth (F/W ratio) may be computed. The concept of net worth has already been examined in some detail under the first (solvency/leverage) ratio. A reference has also been made to the dividing line between fixed and current assets. Here, it appears expedient to dispel the common misconception that fixed assets comprise "land, buildings, plant, machinery, vehicles and furniture". Vehicles, manufactured by an automobile company, for sale, are part of stock-in-trade (current assets) and not fixed assets. Only those vehicles, which are maintained by a firm for being used again and again in the process of production (or for the business of that firm), can be treated as fixed assets. These may include delivery vans used for-the transport of raw materials/finished goods, as also staff cars used by officials/ functionaries for the business of the concerned organization. Vehicles run by a transport undertaking for carrying freight/passenger traffic, too, fall in the category of fixed assets.

Applying the same criterion, furniture and machines manufactured for sale cannot be categorized as fixed assets. Even land and buildings acquired/constructed for sale (as in the case of a land trading company or housing board) cannot pass as fixed assets. Maybe, some firms treat all assets, likely to be retained in business for one year or more, as fixed assets (or, to put it the other way round, all assets, likely to realize within one year, are treated as current assets). These firms may seek to justify such practices on grounds of convenience. But these are, clearly, in violation of the functional rule. Practical convenience, too, is not necessarily assured. In many situations, it may not be clear if a particular asset would jump over the one-year boundary or disappear before the end of the accounting period. If the F/W ratio is greater than unity (>1), it may be interpreted as a sign of weakness from the standpoint of a firm's solvency. The implication is that part of the fixed assets had been financed out of resources not longing to the owners.

Thus, one could visualize the eventuality calling for the liquidation of certain fixed assets for the repayment or redemption of borrowed funds/preference shares. In case the F/W ratio is less than unity (<1), the interpretation would be that part of the net worth is represented by non-fixed (current) assets. This may mean, for the owners some kind of risk emerging from the volatility of current assets. But this is likely to be a safer position for the firm's solvency as judged by its creditors. When the F/W ratio is unity =0, the interests of owners and creditors might stand evenly balanced, provided that there are no serious snags in the basis (bases) of valuation adopted for various items constituting a Balance Sheet. The ratio of "fixed assets to capital employed may be analogous to F/W ratio, if the term "capital employed" is interpreted to mean net worth as discussed earlier user the fourteenth (activity) ratio. A variant of this relationship may be the ratio of "net fixed assets" (gross fixed assets *minus* accumulated depreciation fund) to net worth. Still another variant may be the ratio of "net fixed assets *plus* holdings of industrial securities (investments)" to net worth. The implication of this (latter) variant is that the net worth should fully cover (be represented by) investments in securities also, besides (other) fixed assets, so that there is no pressure to sell these investments (so long as these are sound enough from the stand-points of security and yield).

Seventh, the ratio of capital employed to liabilities may be worked out. It is also called as "proprietor's ratio". If capital employed is interpreted to mean net worth (equity), and liabilities are deemed to be a synonym of debt, this (seventh) ratio would turn out to be a reciprocal of the first (solvency/leverage) ratio. If the proprietor's ratio is greater than unity (>1), it is an index of a firm's solvency (more than full cove-rage of all outside liabilities by the amount of capital employed by owners). In case the proprietors ratio is less than unity (<1), it is a pointer towards a state of insolvency. With this ratio standing at unity (=1), the firm could slip either way as soon as there is a little fluctuation in capital employed or liabilities.

Eighth, the ratio of earnings (net profit before interest and taxes, or EBIT) to interest (fixed interest/dividend obligations) may be worked out. This may be called as "interest coverage ratio", "interest earned", "fixed charge coverage" or "total coverage ratio". The first two of these terms are meant to cover interest only (payable on bonds/debentures/long-term loans/public deposits). As against this, the last two terms mean to cover (besides interest obligations) preference share dividend also. Sometimes, repayment of principal (if required to be made in periodical instalments, or if a sinking fund for redemption of liabilities is called for) may also be included in total coverage.

However, the fact of the matter is that repayment of principal (debt) is not a charge against earnings. As such, a sinking fund (created out of earnings for debt redemption) remains unconsumed after the repayment of particular liability. It may take the form of capital reserve. In any case, it is part of net worth. The same (such as sinking fund) is created only by way of abundant precaution to ensure adequate liquidity. It may be advantageous to work out coverage ratios in respect of several accounting periods/phases of the business cycle, when earnings (EBIT) may be high, medium or low.

These coverage ratios may, then, be read along with the (first) ratio of debt to equity. If the interest on debt is 18 percent, and the debt-equity ratio is 2:1, the minimum level of earnings on permanent capital (equity share capital plus long-term debt) has to be 12 percent as a trade-off between solvency and insolvency. With EBIT standing at nil for three consecutive years, the extent of financial erosion would be 10 percent of the equity share capital, so that the process of becoming insolvent would have more than completed itself. Table 3.4 may be helpful in illustrating the position.

In Table 3.4, the levels of earning on permanent capital (Rs. 300), divided equally between long-term (Rs. 100), reference capital (Rs. 100), and equity capital (Rs. 100) are high (30 percent); medium (18 percent); and low (6 percent).

Table 3.4: Total/Fixed Charge Coverage

		Capital		
S.N	**Type (Amount in Rs.)**	**Medium (Amount) Rs.**	**High (Amount) Rs.**	**Low (Amount) Rs.**
1	Permanent Capital	(300)	90	18
2	Long-Term Capital	(100)	20	20
3	Preference Capital (100)	(100)	1.6	16 (r>)
4	Equity Capital (100)	(100)	54	Nil (!18)

Thus, the interest coverage ratio works out at 4.5 (high (medium) and 0.9 (low) in these three situations. As such in the last phase, part of the interest has to be paid from (owners') capital. The position can be said to be quite good in the first phase, and just satisfactory in the second one. The total/fixed charge coverage ratio, (encompassing interest long-term debt *and* dividend on preference capital) works out at 2.5 (high), 1.5 (medium), and 0.5 (low) in respect of three phases. Thus, preference share dividend (16 percent cannot be paid at all in the third situation'.

Of course, this is generally cumulative and it continues to be a charge on (future) earnings of the firm, so that the same has to be paid in full before declaring any dividend on equity share capital. The total/fixed charge coverage may be said to be satisfactory in respect of the first phase during which equity shareholders are able to get a fairly high dividend of 54 percent. The same would appear to be below the mark in respect of the second phase during which equity shareholders can get a dividend of no more than 18 percent (a rate lower than that of the interest payable on long-term debt, and only marginally higher than the fixed/cumulative rate of dividend available to preference shareholders). Assuming a further dimension that preference shares are to be redeemed after five years, the redemption charge (which, in fact, is not a charge *against* earning/ profit, even though it may be appropriated *out of* the same, in order to discourage the payment of excessive dividend to equity shareholders as a possible danger to the firm's solvency/liquidity) would be Rs. 20 (20 percent) per year. Now, the total\coverage ratio would be about 1.6 (high), less than 1.0 (medium) and only 0.3 (low) for the three phases of the business cycle. During the second phase, the earning is only Rs. 54 as against a total charge of Rs. 56 (quite an unsatisfactory position). As such, only the first phase may be said to have a satisfactory (total) coverage ratio.

Trading on equity is yet another dimension of the coverage ratios. In certain quarters, the process of magnifying the shareholders' return through the employment of debt has been described as "trading on equity" or "leverage". That is, it is trading for the *benefit of equity,* attained *via* the adjustment of capital structure (debt-equity ratio). This is based on the assumption that, the rate of earning (EBIT) is higher than the rate of interest payable on borrowed capital (long-term debt/ creditor ship securities). The greater the edge of EBIT over interest, the better would be the prospect of trading on equity. However, if the rate of earning is lower than the rate of interest, the use of debt will only reduce the rate of dividend available to equity shareholders. This is well in evidence in the last phase of the cycle as depicted in Table 3.4. Here, the meagre earning of 6 percent on permanent capital does not suffice even for fixed annual obligations (interest on long-term debt and dividend on preference share capital).

Trading on capital may also help the equity shareholders in controlling much larger funds with a relatively small volume of investment (since holders of creditor ship securities/public deposits, normally, do not have the power of voting/decision-making). Where the interest coverage ratio is good enough even in the lean period, and the rate of earning is very much higher than the rate of interest during a period of boom, there may be tremendous possibility of escalating the rate of dividend on equity shareholders by augmenting the proportion of debt more and more. Thus, in Table 3.4, if the amount of long-term debt is pushed up to Rs. 800 (with permanent capital going up to Rs. 1,000), the earning (EBIT) would be Rs. 300. After paying Rs. 160 as interest on long-term debt and Rs. 16 as dividend on preference capital, the balance of Rs 124 would be able to provide a dividend as high as 124 percent on, equity capital (even though the rate of earning is only 30 percent) during the boom period.

Ninth, the ratio of debt servicing (annual repayment *plus* interest *plus* preference dividend) to annual fund (profit *plus* depreciation *plus* interest) may be worked out. Here, the numerator (debt servicing) is analogous to the denominator (total coverage) as referred to under the eighth ratio. The denominator of ninth ratio (annual fund) is profit before charging depreciation. As such, it is different from the numerator (EBIT) in respect of the eighth ratio. The ratio of debt servicing to annual fund (ninth ratio) goes to indicate the extent to which current revenue is getting dissipated in the fulfilment of past obligations. As such, it can be a valuable guideline, or even a warning bell, relevant to debt negotiations and capital structure decisions of today, which are likely to influence/mortgage the earnings/cash flows of tomorrow. In particular, such a ratio may be of great significance in formulating/reshaping macro-economic policies, such as those relating to public debt, in the context of both national and international dimensions.

For example, the World Development Report, 1984 pointed out: "Concern about creditworthiness is related both to the likelihood that debtors, if necessary, will be willing to service their debt out of income (rather than extra borrowing) and to the economic cost of debt service. The cost depends on several factors: the ratio of debt to wealth (in the case of a country, the present value of future national income); the real rate of interest; the ease with which the necessary adjustments to spending in relation to output can be made; and the cost of making transfers in foreign exchange".

The debt service ratio, as calculated by the World Bank, is the ratio of "interest payments *plus* amortization" to exports. With its fall in 1974 (as against 1970), possibly in the wake of oil price hike which immediately boosted up the exports of oil-rich developing countries, the debt service burden stood at less than one-tenth of the export earnings. By 1983, it had shot up to more than one-fifth of such earnings, thus signifying an alarming deterioration in the creditworthiness of developing countries as a group. In particular, Mexico could not service its debt in August 1982, on account of short maturities and high nominal interest rates. Subsequently, a number of countries faced debt servicing difficulties and, in 1983, there were 36 rescheduling involving US$ 67 million of debt (over 11 percent of total debt). Between 1970 and 1982, the debt service ratio had gone up from 12.5 percent to 42.1 percent for Brazil, from 6.8 percent to, 36.9 percent for Ivory Coast, and from 7.7 percent to 36.8 percent for Morocco.

Thus, roughly two-fifths of the export earnings stood mortgaged for meeting external debt obligations (interest and amortization) of such countries. The rise in interest payments (alone) was much faster, from US$ 133 million to US$ 5,896 million for Brazil, from US$ 11 million to US$ 476 million for Ivory Coast, and from US$ 23 million to US$ 615 million for Morocco. The ratio of external public debt to GNP, as also the ratio of debt to exports, roughly doubled itself between 1974 and 1983. A few countries had their ratio of debt to GNP higher than 100 percent. The amount of total debt (of developing countries) in 1983 was more than four times the figure obtaining in 1974. Thus, both GNP and exports could not rise as fast as the amount of debt during 1974-83; for, if the rise were commensurate, the ratios would have remained constant. The ratio of interest service to GNP was rising all along. In 1983, it stood at a point more than three times the level obtained in 1974, and more than four times the 1970 benchmark. This is partly explained by the fact that private debt (associated, usually, with high commercial rates of interest) rose much faster than official debt (often associated with concessional rates of interest). The ratio of official debt to private debt was roughly 1:1 in 1970 and1:2 in 1983.

Tenth, the ratio of "total debt (short-term and long-term) plus (redeemable) preference share capital" to "annual fund (profit plus depreciation plus interest)" may be computed. Here, the numerator covers all such liabilities which may have to be paid back (now or later) during the lifetime of a company. That is, only equity share capital (which, normally, cannot be returned to the owners, except in the event of winding up/liquidation) is excluded on this score. This ratio seeks to answer the question: How many years annual fund (or how many times the annual fund) would suffice to pay off all debt and redeemable capital? The resulting figure (ratio) has to be interpreted keeping in view the rate of interest and the period of maturity. The lower the ratio (as also, the lower the rate of interest on debt) and the longer the period of maturity, the better it might be for the firm's solvency. Thus, if the ratio is three (3), the rate of interest is 10 percent, and the period of maturity is fifteen (15) years, the position would appear to be quite safe.

Eleventh, the ratio of total debt (which may not include preference capital) to "operating cash flow" (OCF or earnings after interest and taxation) or "cash flow" (CF or net income *plus* depreciation, depletion and amortization) may be computed. Here, the numerator may be the same as with the tenth ratio. But the denominator in respect of the eleventh ratio (OCF) may be very much lower (after deducting interest and taxation from earnings) than the one appearing in respect of the tenth ratio (annual fund). As such, the ratio of total debt to OCF is likely to be substantially higher than the ratio of total debt to annual fund. In other words, the eleventh ratio seeks to establish a more rigorous requirement as a test of solvency, presuming that the same figure (say 3) is still considered as the desired norm. Accordingly, it would call for much greater effort to have an OCF of that magnitude. The rationale behind such rigor is that interest and taxation are such burdens which cannot, normally, be avoided or postponed. It is only the dividend on (equity) share capital which may be said to be of a discretionary character. As such, the real cushion for repayment of debt (out of earnings) may appear to be OCF rather than annual fund.

Twelfth, the ratio of long-term debt to net working capital (after adjusting short-term loans) may be worked out. It is different from the seventh (liquidity) ratio not only in respect of the changed position of net working capital (from numerator to denominator), but also with regard to the smaller coverage of long-term debt as compared to all long-term funds. If this twelfth (solvency/leverage) ratio is less than unity (<1), it would imply that the long-term debt is fully covered by net current assets, so that the eventuality of selling fixed assets (for the redemption of such debt) would not arise. In case the ratio is greater than unity (>1), it might be interpreted to mean insufficient coverage of long-term debt and some kind of hazard for the firm's solvency. If the long-term debt is in the form of public deposits, the aforesaid conclusion based on the ratio of such debt to net working capital may be quite pertinent.

The tests of solvency/leverage ratios discussed above do not constitute an exhaustive list. It is possible to think of many other relationships on this score. Some of these may appear analogous to liquidity and activity ratios examined earlier. Mentioned below are a few examples:

(a) ratio of all bank borrowings (current liabilities) to total assets *(thirteenth),* a vital test of solvency (measuring the thickness of overall cushion) which any lending institution (short-term or long-term) may like to apply while considering a loan application or request for overdraft/cash credit;

(b) ratio of all bank borrowings to sales *(fourteenth),* a

measure of solvency which seeks to supplement the earlier one by viewing the cushion in the context of the borrowing firm's current level of activity (which has a vital bearing on the level of total assets likely to obtain in future);

(c) ratio of interest (or interest *plus* amortization) to sales, gross or net of excise *(fifteenth),* which seeks to view leverage/coverage of annual charge (debt servicing) in the context of a firm's current level of performance (activity) in the marketing area;

(d) ratio of net fixed assets to gross fixed assets *(sixteenth),* which can be a useful supplement: to certain other solvency tests for ascertaining the asset condition (qualitative dimension) in the context of a (borrowing) firm's policy with regard to depreciation, obsolescence, replacement, and valuation of fixed assets (which provide long-term cushion for debt); and

(e) ratio of current liabilities to not worth *(seventeenth),* which may be in the nature of an (inverse) index of a firm's ability (cushion against owners' fund) to meet long-term debt obligations (after settling current liabilities), so that the lower this ratio the higher might be the level of solvency (long-term liquidity).

3.4 Profitability Ratios

The word "profit" has had French/Latin origin in "proficere" (being useful or proficient), "profectus" and "profectum" (to make progress). Thus, profit is an index of proficiency or progress, as typified by "the gain resulting from the employment of capital" (and/or risk-taking), "the excess of returns over expenditure; pecuniary gain in any transaction/occupation" (activity), or "the difference between the selling price and the first cost; the sum remaining after all costs are deducted from the income of a business". Sometimes, distinction is made as follows between three concepts of income/profit (under conditions of certainty):

(a) Economic income=any change over the period in the

capitalized value of dividends of this and future periods;

(b) Tangible income=economic income—change in value of goodwill over the period=total change in the value of tangible equity; and

(c) Accounting income=tangible income—change in value of tangible assets not realized in this period changes in value of tangible assets accrued in other periods and realized in this period=proceeds of all assets sold—costs assigned to these assets.

Under conditions of uncertainty, economic income essentially rests on an *estimation* of the present value of the *expectation* regarding future net receipts. That is, the expected net cash inflows (excess of recurring cash inflows over recurring cash outflows connected with the operations) are subjected to an appropriate rate of discount (which may stand determined by 'the rate of interest, rate of inflation/deflation, and/or other relevant variables). According to Professor Bounding, "the difference in outlook of economists and accountants is perhaps, one of emphasis rather than of principle. The accountant asks himself simply how profitable is the enterprise; the economist asks himself how profitable it might have been if it had done something different, and especially what it would have to do in order to make maximum profits ... in more mathematical language, the economist is interested in the balance-sheet as a vector in w-space. The accountant is interested in reducing this n-dimensional vector to a simple scalar that is a single number".

An important point of difference between the accountant's approach and the economic (concept of) profit might be in respect of imputed costs which in the latter case, are deducted (in addition to money outlays) from the (wherein, too, imputation may be part of the economist's exercise). In economics, profit is regarded as the income which accrues to the entrepreneur, i.e. the residual left after payment of all opportunity costs to the inputs he employs. Two types of profit are usually talked about. "Normal profit" is defined as that profit which is just sufficient to induce the entrepreneur to remain in his present activity. Profit over and above normal profit is referred to as "pure profit", "excess profit" 'or "super normal profit".

Accounting, too, distinguishes between two types of profit. "Gross profit" represents the excess of gross (operational) revenue over the costs *directly* incurred in carrying on the operations of a firm. "Net profit" is arrived after deducting, from gross profit, *indirect* costs (such as interest o loan and depreciation), and after adding thereto non-operations revenue (like interest earned on bank accounts). It is the residual figure after meeting all the relevant costs. If the total cost exceeds total revenues, there would be "net loss". The surplus which remains after deducting tax (income tax, excess profit tax, corporation tax, or such other direct tax) is the profit available for distribution (payment of dividend) and reinvestment (in the form of reserve fund).

Profitability is the capacity of an organization/activity to earn profits in the normal course of operation. Thus, an inefficient firm, which makes large profits on account of fortuitous circumstances (such as sudden price rise/stockpiling programme in the wake of a war), would not, in strict terms, pass as profitable. On the other hand, an efficient undertaking which suffers loss accidentally (say, resulting from an earthquake) may still be deemed as profitable. However, in actual practice it may be quite difficult to abide by such an abstract definition distinction. Perhaps, it may be more convenient to say the profitability refers to a situation where (the value of) output exceeds (the cost of) input (no matter whether such a situation is normal or only accidental). In other words, profitability follows "overall contribution". Profits per rupee/pound sterling/dollar of sales, as such, could be a measure of profitability. A convenient device for analyzing profitability is a "normalize income statement" in which all items are expressed as one for the purpose of giving serial numbers to various profitability ratios (though a beginning is being made with a few of the sales-based ratios as emerging from normalized income statement, while some other ratios relevant to this statement may be taken up later on).

First, the ratio of gross operating profit (before deducting depreciation/indirect expense) to sales may be calculated. This is known as "gross operating margin" or "gross profit margin". It may also be worked out by deducting cost of goods sold from sales and, then, dividing the remainder by sales. If it is proposed to express this ratio as a percentage, the figure so arrived at may be multiplied by 100. It has been revealed that the gross (operating) profit margin fell from 45 percent in 1984 to 43 percent is a 1985. This is an evidence of the (reduced) proficiency with which direct costs, relevant to a particular level of output/sales, being managed/controlled. Further, introspection, through a series of subordinate ratios, goes to reveal that the most uncontrollable factor was direct labour cost which experienced maximum escalation (from 15.5 percent to 17.5 percent).

As against this, the most effective control (maximum economy) would appear to have manifested itself in respect of factory overhead (whose ratio to sales actually fell from 12 percent to 11 percent). Raw material cost may be said to represent the middle range on the score of proficiency in control, its ratio to sales having gone up from 27.5 percent to 28.5 percent. However, a word of caution is called for in the interpretation of such ratios. Any increase in cost/cost ratio does not necessarily imply managerial inefficiency/ ineffectiveness. Wages, prices and other elements of cost may have gone up on account of external (or even internal) factors well beyond the control of management. In fact, it may even be that costs of the firm under study have escalated much less than what some (other) competing/comparable firms have experienced during the same span of time. If so, the management of that particular firm may deserve a pat on the back in spite of some cost escalation. By the same token, any decrease in cost/cost ratio does not, necessarily, entitle the management team to get a certificate of merit. It may be that some competing/comparable firms have been able to effect greater economies (than the firm under reference) on account of downswing in prices/wages, technological change and such other variables. If so, the management of this particular firm may, justifiably, be censured not with standing some decrease in costs.

Second, the ratio of cost of goods sold (cost of sales/direct costs) to sales may be computed. There is complementarily between this ratio and the first one. If the gross profit margin is 0.45 (45 percent), the direct costs ratio would be 0.55 (55 percent). On the same basis, if the direct costs ratio is 0.57 (57 percent), the gross profit margin would be 0.43 (43 percent). Three ratios subordinate to the direct costs ratio is the ratio of cost of goods sold to sales) have already been referred to in the earlier paragraph. One can think of many other such (subordinate/descendant) ratios. It may be relevant to revert to these ratios at a later stage.

Third the ratio of (net) operating profit (after deducting depreciation/indirect expense, but before deducting interest/ tax) to sales may be computed. This ratio fell from 28 percent in 1984 to 27 percent in 1985, thus indicating a little fall in the level of profitability. However, the magnitude of this fall is marginally less than that experienced by the ratio of gross (operating) profit to sales. This slight improvement is accountable to substantial economy in indirect expense (such economy having more than counterbalanced the somewhat increased burden of depreciation). A variant of this relationship may be the ratio of "net profit" or cash flow to sales or "net sales".

Fourth, the ratio of depreciation to sales may be calculated. This, ratio went- up from 2.2 percent in 1984 to 2.4 percent in 1985. An increase in such a ratio goes to erode profitability. In this case, the overall magnitude of depreciation is relatively small. But, in case of high technology/capital intensive industries (say, in respect of aircraft, deployed for civil aviation by a commercial airline, or the spacecraft, if and when it enters the phase of commercial feasibility), the rate of depreciation to sales may be quite high. Besides that, the burden of obsolescence may also be quite heavy on account of rapid innovations, as also due to the extremely low tolerance limit in respect of technical defect which come to light in equipment used for highly sophisticate and delicate operations of this kind. If necessary, several ratios subordinate to the ratio of depreciation to sales may also be worked out. These subordinate ratios may be in respect several fixed assets, such as buildings, office/factory premises furniture/fixtures, plant/machinery, transport vehicles, and other equipment. It may be relevant to revert to these ratios later on.

Fifth, the ratio of indirect expenses to sales may t worked out. This ratio fell perceptibly from 14.8 percent in 1984 to 13.6 percent in 1985, this improving the prospect of profitability. However, the behaviour of three subordinate ratios in respect of office, marketing are general expenses was not uniform. The ratio of general expense to sales remained constant at 4.8 percent. As against the office expenses rose marginally from 4.4 percent to 4.6 percent while marketing expenses fell substantially from 5.6 percent 4.2 percent. If a still deeper probe is desired, descendant ratio for each one of these subordinate ratios can be worked out. It may be relevant to revert to such ratios at a later stage. Here it may only be added that the fourth ratio (in respect of depreciation) and the fifth ratio (relating to indirect expense) a complementary to the first ratio (gross profit margin) and to third ratio (net operating margin). That is, net operating pro is arrived at after deducting depreciation and indirect expense from gross profit.

Sixth, the ratio of "cost of goods sold *plus* operating expenses (depreciation/indirect expenses) to sales may be calculated. It is commonly known as the "operating ratio". The special context of railways and other transport undertaking the same has also been described as the "transportation ratio to which reference was made in the previous section (while tracking the growth of ratio analysis as a tool of management). The operating ratio rose from 72 percent (55.0+2.2+14.8) in 1984 to 73 percent (57.0+2.4+13.6) in 1999. It is complementary to the (net) operating profit margin (third ratio) which fell from 28 percent to 27 percent. That is, the third and sixth ratios would add up to 100 percent. In other words, a rise "in the operating ratio impinges on the profitability of an undertaking. With an operating ratio of 100 percent, the (net) operating profit would be reduced to zero; and, when the former touches 110 percent, there would be a (net) operating loss of 10 percent (on sales).

These are not imaginary situations, since railways/airways/roadways have been forced to operate with low/nil/negative profit margins in many situations emerging from the "social purpose content" of public ownership/interest and/or the irreversibility of fixed capital investment (even when private ownership has the option to withdraw). For example, tramways in Bombay, during the last few years of their operation (before this mode of city transport stood finally suspended), had experienced sharp decline in traffic, so much so that a tram, running with only two persons inside (the driver and the conductor on duty, with no paying passengers), was not an unusual sight. Sometimes, the decline in traffic is qualitative and not quantitative as such. For example, with the phenomenal growth of road transport in independent India, a substantial part of high class goods traffic stood diverted from the (publicly owned) Indian Railways to (private) road transport operators. Likewise, the operating ratio of a manufacturing, enterprise may rise or fall with every change in its product-mix, (proportionate shares of several products sold at varying, gross margins) or its input-mix (proportionate shares of various types of raw materials/labour/other inputs). Changes in the price/output policy, wage/salary structure, depreciation policy, and overheads/other operating expenses may as well affect a firm's operating ratio. Accordingly, an exclusive reliance on this ratio as a barometer of efficiency may not be advisable, particularly in the case of multi-plant and multi-product firms, the broad picture emerging from the behaviour of operating, ratio has to be reviewed with the help of various subordinate ratios and other information of a critical character.

Seventh, the ratio of profit before tax (PBT) to sales may be computed. PBT is arrived at after deducting (net) interest from (net) operating profit. In many cases, only "interest payable" is taken into account. But, if there is some interest receivable, the same should also be taken into account. In fact, the possibility of the latter exceeding the former cannot be ruled out, even though such a situation may be rare (say, when lot of surplus funds get invested outside the firm, which may be passing through a prolonged lean period). The ratio of PBT to sales fell from 25.0 percent in 1984 to 22.5 percent in 1985. This index reveals maximum decline in profitability, much greater than that visible in (net) operating profit (which fell from 28 percent to" 27 percent). The gulf was widened by the phenomenal escalation in (net) interest burden.

Eighth, the ratio of interest (net) to sales may be worked out. It jumped up from 3.0 percent in 1984 to 4.5 percent in 1985. Here, two subordinate ratios have-also been computed. The ratio of interest payable to sales had a steep rise from 4.1 percent to 5.4 percent, thus making for a substantial fall in profitability. The ratio of interest receivable to sales displayed a decline (though not as fast) from 1.1 percent to 0.9 percent. This further aggravated the fall in profitability. If the second subordinate ratio had gone up, it could have compensated (to some extent) the increased burden emanating from the rise in the first subordinate ratio. The crux of the situation is that interest payable is to be deducted from (net) operating profit, whereas interest receivable is to be added to such profit. If, besides interest receivable, there is any other non-operating income, the same has to be dealt with in a similar fashion. By the same token, any non-operating expenditure besides interest payable has to be deducted from (net) operating profit.

Ninth, the ratio of profit after tax (If AT) to sales may be calculated. PAT is arrived at after deducting, from PBT, direct taxes on income/profit, such as income tax, corporation tax and excess profits tax. If, according to law of the land, a company has to pay other direct taxes, such as wealth tax and gift tax, these, too, may have to be taken into account. The taxes falling in this latter category may be of particular significance when profitability ratios are worked out on the basis of assets/investment (as denominator). PAT declined from 15.0 percent in 1984 to 13.5 percent in 1985. This fall was of a smaller magnitude than that experienced in respect of PBT. The gulf stood narrowed down on account of a somewhat lower burden of tax which, by its very nature, slips down along with a lower level of profitability. The ratio of PAT to sales is also known as "net profit margin" (available for distribution).

Tenth, the ratio of tax to sales may be calculated. Here the focus is on direct taxes only (which vary with the amount of income/profit or wealth/investment). So far as indirect taxes are concerned, these are appropriately taken into account along with the cost of materials/inputs and indirect expense. However, the treatment of sales tax, which does not form part of the operating cost as such, may mean some difficulty. Yet, this matter is of particular significance when profitability ratios are worked out on the basis of sales (as denominator). Firms whose sales do not exceed the statutory exemption limit are not required to pay sales tax (and, as such, are not entitled to charge the same from customers). As against, this, customers may have to pay more for the same products bought from firms whose total sales in an accounting period are higher than the prescribed exemption limit. And the same firm may be subject to sales tax in one accounting period, while it may not be so in another such period. So, it becomes difficult to make comparative assessment of profitability.

One of the situations may be that sales tax is being realized (on the one, hand) and an equivalent amount is being deposited with the taxing authority (on the other). Here, it may be best to ignore the element of sales tax altogether (both for numerator and for denominator). In a second situation, the amount of sales tax realised from customers may be less than what is required to be paid, to government. Here, it may form part of indirect expense, since the payment of this amount is not contingent upon the making of profit. In a third situation, a firm may have recovered more (by way of sales tax) than what it is called upon to deposit with the tax office. This may appear queer; but, surprisingly, several sales tax laws seemed to permit this situation through some kind of a "mixing up" between selling price and cost price as bases of realizing and depositing tax (on the part of an assessed firm). Here, sales tax could mean net gain to the firm which may be adjusted against indirect expense (just as interest receivable is adjusted against interest payable, somewhat different lines). The ratio of tax to has gone down from 10 percent to 9 percent. The presumption is that PBT (which itself has declined from 25.0 percent 1984 to 22.5 percent in 1985) is subjected to direct tax flat rate (implicitly assumed to be 40 percent in this case).

All the ten profitability ratios, worked out on the basis of sales as denominator, and discussed above, are re-computed with total assets/investment or net worth or debt as base (denominator). The numerator can also be different say "net income" or cash flow (net income plus depreciation depletion, and amortization). Thus, the tally may include:

net income to sales;
net income to total assets;
net income to net worth;
net income to total debt;
cash flow to sales;
cash flow to total assets;
cash flow to net worth; and
cash flow to total debt.

As such, repeat exercises may appear superfluous. However a continuation of the serial with some variants may be while.

Eleventh, the ratio of (net) operating profit (earnings) after deducting depreciation/indirect expense, but before calculating the interest/tax, (i.e. EBIT to total gross investment and assets plus gross operating fixed assets) may be calculated, ratio may be known as "productivity of assets" (POA), "on investment" (ROI), or "earning power". Sometimes, depreciation is not deducted from (net) operating profit (or, depreciation is added back to such profit) for determining the sum while working out this ratio. Such a procedure is advocated with a view to getting away from the elements of discrete volatility associated with depreciation policies, which impede fair comparisons of profitability between competing firms or, in respect of the same firm, between several accounting periods during an era of rapid price change. Moreover, it can be argued that, if depreciation is deducted from the numerator, the cumulative figure of depreciation should be deducted from the denominator also. That is, net fixed assets (instead of gross fixed assets) should be added to current assets for determining the total level of investment (serving as base for this profitability ratio). A further variant of the denominator may be to take only net current assets (current assets *minus* current liabilities) into account.

Twelfth, the ratio of incremental (net) operating profit to incremental investment may be computed. It may be described as "marginal productivity of assets" (MPOA). However, the application of this concept in actual practice may give queer results. It may be found in several situations that, with an increase in investment, profit has actually declined. That is, the numerator may be a negative figure, while the denominator is a positive one. Likewise, it may be discovered that, with a fall in the level of investment, profit has actually risen. That is, the numerator may be positive, while the denominator is a negative figure. Some such situations may be the product of changing business/political environment. In any case, a great deal of caution is called for in applying the incremental ratios. Assuming practical proposition, the unit of (incremental) investment, used as denominator, has to be fairly big in order to appear significant. Moreover, investments made at different points of time, and at widely varying price levels, have to be brought to some common ground for purposes of comparison. Likewise, the profits, as worked out for different accounting periods, should have a fairly common (comparable) basis of computation.

Another dimension of this ratio may be the physical capacity/ technological sophistication of the new equipment in relation to that obtaining in respect of the existing equipment. This aspect of the matter may not get the focus which it deserves when only financial figures of investment are taken into account. For example, the cost of an aircraft capable of carrying 500 passengers is not, necessarily, four times that of another aircraft which can accommodate 125 passengers only (even if the changes in price level were ignored). In fact, even the carrying capacities of two types of aircraft may not be in such precise multiples as stated above. Moreover, the spans of working life, standards of fuel consumption/maintenance, and other technical details can be so divergent that a financial ratio, by itself, may not be of much account. It can actually present quite a deceptive picture, specially when the initial capacity utilization of any large-sized equipment is rather low. As such, a more practical proposition may be to prepare an "income variability index" (either on a base which remains fixed for a number of years, or on a chain base shifting from year to year). Something of this nature (variability of profitability over time) was worked out by James A. Ohlson in "Financial Ratios and the Probabilistic Prediction of Bankruptcy" *(Journal of Accounting Research,* Spring, 1980). The last one of the nine variables taken into account in "Ohlson Model" could be spelt out as follows:

$CHIN = (NI,-NI_{t}-_{1})/(NI_{l}+NIt+_{1})$

where,

CHIN stands for change in net income,

NI, is net income for the most recent period,

NIt-1 is net income for the period immediately preceding the most recent period, and

NIt+1 is (anticipated) net income for the period immediately following the most recent period.

The "stability of ratios" may, further, be tested on the basis of standard-deviation/coefficient of variation.

Thirteenth, the ratio of net income or profit after tax (PAT) to shareholders' equity (net worth) may be worked out. The denominator may cover ordinary share capital (common stock), preference share capital, share premium, reserves and surplus (less accumulated loss, if any). However, such an interpretation may fail to indicate the precise profitability from the standpoint of equity shareholders. This is so because preference shares, usually, are entitled only to a fixed dividend (unless these are participating preference shares). As such, it may be appropriate to deduct preference share dividend from profit after tax for working out a profitability ratio meaningful for equity shareholders.

This is, sometimes called as "productivity of equity block". It may be the ratio of *"PAT plus* depreciation *minus* preference dividend" to "equity paid up *plus* reserves *plus* accumulated depreciation." This is a variant of the "return on shareholders' equity" (ROSL) discussed earlier. The logic of adding current depreciation to the numerator, along with that of adding accumulated depreciation to the denominator, has been referred to under the eleventh ratio. Another variant of ROSE may be the ratio of profit before tax (PBT) to net worth. All these relationships are very vital for most firms interested either in maximizing the return on owners' investment or, at least, in maintaining profit at a satisfactory level. This rate of return can be compared with other competing/comparable firms (or the industry/area average), as also with the rates of return obtained by that very firm in earlier accounting periods. Of course, while scrutinizing such ratios, the prevailing political/business environment (both external and internal) has to be kept in view for arriving at judicious findings.

Fourteenth, the ratio of (net) income, profit or earnings (EBDIT/EBIT/OCF) to total assets (or tangible assets) may be calculated. It is called the "return on assets" (ROA) or "profit-to-assets ratio". With total assets as the denominator, the underlying assumption is that all assets (including intangibles) must contribute (directly or indirectly) to a firm's profit/ earning. So to say in the absence of such a contribution, there is no economic justification of acquiring/building up/maintaining an asset. As such, patents and copyrights (appearing as assets in a Balance Sheet) which do not contribute to profit, must be written. In fact, the ROA may ever cast a reflection on the wisdom of acquiring such assets, in case their contribution to profit was nil (or negligible) from the very beginning. Likewise, deferred revenue expenditure (such as massive advertising), appearing as an asset in the Balance Sheet, must (continue to) contribute to the profit-earning capacity of the firm concerned. Similarly, if there is over-investment in fixed and/or current assets, the same may get reflected in ROA. This part of the function, however, could as well be performed by the eleventh ratio (productivity of assets or POA) in respect of which the denominator comprised current and operating fixed assets *only,* as against *all* the assets constituting the denominator under the fourteenth ratio (ROA). The following are some of the variants of ROA:

ratio of "earnings-before-depreciation-interest-and-taxation" (EBDIT) to total assets (with or without accumulated depreciation);

ratio of "earnings-before-interest-and-taxation" (EBIT) to total assets (with or without accumulated depreciation).

ratio of "earnings-after-interest-and-taxation-with depreciation provision added back" (operating cash flow or OCF) to "total assets *plus* accumulated depreciation" *(of* total assets without adding back accumulated depreciation, although such a definition of denominator could not be in line with the numerator to which depreciation provision has been added back).

Fifteenth, the ratio of profit before tax (PBT) or profit after tax (PAT) to capital employed may be worked out. It is known as "return on capital employed" (ROCE). The term capital employed can be interpreted in a number of ways. If capital employed stands for "total assets", ROCE would be the same thing as ROA (fourteenth profitability ratio discussed above). In case capital employed appears as a synonym of net worth, ROCE may not be different from ROSE (thirteenth profitability ratio discussed earlier). However, there may be leveral variants of ROCE itself. Some of these are indicated below (the denominator being fundamentally different in the last description):

ratio of "net profit after taxes *plus* interest" to capital employed;

ratio of "net profit after taxes *plus* interest *plus* depreciation" to capital employed;

ratio of "gross (operating) profit (net profit after taxes *plus* interest *plus* depreciation *plus* indirect expenses)" to capital employed;

ratio of "net profit after taxes *plus* interest" to "capital employed *minus* intangible assets"; and

ratio of net income to net working capital.

Sixteenth, the ratio of "present value of inflows" to outlay (initial cash outflow, or present value of all cash outflows/ investment) may be worked out. It is known as "profitability index" (PI). If the ratio is unity (=1), profitability stands at zero level; that is there is neither profit nor loss (the present value of future benefits being just equal to that of investment). In case PI) is greater than unity (>1), profitability is positive. The relative margin of profit is measured by the extent to which PI exceeds 1. Thus, a PI of 1.20 symbolizes profitability to the tune of 20 percent on investment. When PI is less than unity (<1), profitability is negative (that is, there is loss). Thus, if PI is 0.90, there is a loss of 10 percent on investment. Future cash inflows are discounted at an appropriate rate of interest/ discount, which may have some relationship with the rate of interest available on fixed deposits (at a certain point of time for a specified period). If outlays/investment/cash outflows have accrued at different points of time, these too may have to be converted to the present value through a similar process of discounting.

This procedure (whether applied to inflows or outflows) is known as "time adjustment". A further procedure of "price level adjustment" (inflation/revaluation accounting) may call for indexation of various amounts/figures in terms of real value. As such, there may be two-fold discounting (for interest and inflation respectively). Thus, if rate of interest/discount, is 10 percent, and the annual rate of inflation is 25 percent, the present value of a future cash inflow (due after one year) of Rs. 110 would be Rs. 80 only. Here the effective rate of interest (in-real terms) turns out to be negative. This is bound to be so when the rate of inflation is higher than the rate of interest. Thus, the nominal/money value of Rs. 100 invested at 10 percent interest would be Rs. 110 after one year. But the real value would actually fall (in terms of price level obtaining at the time of initial investment) to Rs. 88 (dividing 110 by 125, and then multiplying the resultant figure by 100). In a contrary situation, where prices are falling (the real value of money is rising), the effective rate of interest (in real terms) would appear to be higher than the nominal rate.

With price index falling from 100 to 80 during the aforesaid period, the real value of Rs. 100 invested at 10 percent rate of interest would be (as against the nominal value of Rs. 110) as high as Rs. 137 or 138 (dividing 110 by 80, and then multiplying the resultant figure by 100). So, the rate of interest, in real terms, would be over 37 percent. Even if the nominal rate of interest were nil or zero, the real value of Rs. 100 would rise to Rs. 125 (when the price index falls from 100 to 80), thus revealing an interest (or profit) in real terms to the tune of 25 percent. However, this process of indexation tends to be quite complicated; and a proposal to introduce the same in India's Seventh Five Year Plan (1985-1990) was rejected by the National Development Council (November 1985). The experience of a few other countries (which launched this experiment), too, did not turn out to be happy (on the whole). As such, in spite of its serious limitations in an era of rapid price change, discounting has been done usually for time adjustment only, and not for inflation adjustment.

The same thing applies to "benefit-cost ratio", which is just another version of "profitability index", so long as only monetary benefits and monetary costs are taken into account. That is, a project is deemed viable only if B/C ratio is greater than unity (>1). When B/C ratio is unity (=1), it is indicative of a break-even position. In case B/C ratio is Jess than unity (< 1), a project is not likely to be taken up, unless there are overriding considerations of personal prestige, social welfare or political necessity. Where such considerations prevail, certain non-monetary benefits (psychological/political/social) have been *implicitly* taken into account. In a contrary situation, the B/C ratio of a project, as measured by monetary parameters, may be quite high; and, yet, the project may not be taken up because of psychological, political and social barriers'(non-monetary costs, such as those typified by environmental pollution or ecological imbalance). For example, the B/C ratio of cutting down a young forest may appear to be quite profitable in a narrow commercial sense; but, in a broad social perspective, such an activity may turn out to be suicidal. As such, the ratio of social benefit to social cost is of great relevance, particularly for public sector projects. In fine, a more comprehensive view of the situation can be obtained by working out the ratio of "commercial benefit *plus* social benefit" to "commercial cost plus social cost." Of course, the process of "adding up" these two types of benefit on the one hand, and the two types of cost on the other, may encounter serious problems of valuation.

Seventeenth, the ratio of contribution (fixed cost *plus* net profit) to sales may be calculated. It is known as profit volume (P/V) ratio. The same can be defined as the ratio of variable margin (excess of sales/revenue over variable costs) to sales. The P/V ratio is a constant percentage which can be used to ascertain the amount of profit at any level of output/sales. As such, it can also be stated as the ratio of "contribution per unit" to "sales price per unit". Likewise, this relationship can be described as the ratio of "incremental contribution (in respect of profit)" to "incremental sales". For example, 'if the level of profit is Rs. 2,000 on a sales volume of Rs. 20,000, and Rs. 4,000 on a sales volume of Rs. 30,000, the P/V ratio works out at 20 percent (the numerator being Rs. 4,000-2,000 =2,000, while the denominator is Rs. 30,000-20,000=10,000). On the basis of this ratio, the fixed cost is found to be Rs. 2,000. The contribution (fixed cost *plus* profit), being 20 percent of sales, works out to Rs. 4,000 on a sales, volume of Rs. 20,000, and Rs. 6,000 on a sales volume of Rs. 30,000. Whether an amount of Rs. 2000 (profit at a sales volume of Rs. 20,000) is deducted from' Rs. 4,000, or a sum of Rs. 4,000 (profit at a sales volume of Rs: 30,000) is deducted from Rs. 6,000, the remainder (fixed cost) is Rs. 2,000.

If the selling price per unit is taken to be Rs. 10, the volume of sales would appear at 2,000 and 3,000 units in these two situations respectively. The contribution per unit would, then, be two rupees, whereas the variable cost would appear at eight rupees per unit. Further, the break-even point sales can be arrived at (Rs. 10,000), if fixed cost (Rs. 2,000) is divided by P/V ratio (20 percent or one-fifth). In case it is desired to earn a particular amount of profit (say, Rs. 5,000), the P/V ratio can be helpful in finding out the level of sales (Rs 35,000) at which that level of profit is likely to be obtained. This figure is arrived at by adding the desired profit to fixed cost and then dividing this total amount by P/V ratio. The amount of profit likely to be earned at a particular level of sales (say Rs. 40,000) can also be worked out with the help of P/V ratio, by deducting the fixed cost (Rs. 2,000) from the contribution (20 percent or Rs. 8,000 at a sales volume of Rs. 40,000), the amount of profit (Rs. 6,000) relevant to the particular level of sales is ascertained.

Sometimes, certain "intervals" based on "fun expenditures for operations" or FEO (operating expenses *mini* depreciation, depletion and amortization) are also uncertain. These intervals, represent some sort of a twilight zone between profitability and liquidity (possibly, along with activity of solvency). *First,* the ratio of cash to FEO may be described; "cash interval". If this ratio stands at 0.08 (8 percent), implies that a firm has enough cash balance to meet (day-to-day operating expenses for 29 days (about a month or four week only (assuming that no such expense is incurred on credit). In other words, if there is no inflow of cash during this period, the firm's business would come to a standstill after the expiry "cash interval". It is a kind *of breathing space* for enabling the firm to replenish its (anticipated) cash depletions. The long this interval, the more comfortable a firm may feel, so as it avoid the dangers of cash management on a *crash basis* (high rates of interest and other exacting conditions so common associated with the *modus operandi* of indigenous bankers in India).

However, on the other hand, the longer the cash interval, to higher is the cost of maintaining idle cash (besides the hazards of extravagance-pilferage and misappropriation in a "surplus cash situation"). As such, a high ratio of cash to FEO is an indication of poor financial planning. That is, the firm gets "away" from the norm of "zero cash balance" (ideal cash management). As a practical proposition, both a lower limit at a higher limit may be relevant to cash interval in the context a particular situation. *Secondly,* the concept may be widened, that the ratio of defensive assets (quick assets) to FEO may be described as "defensive interval".

Here, the numerator covers (besides cash) other quick assets also (mainly receivables). This, the firm can look to realizations from trade debtors as a fair definite source of cash inflow in view of the commercial convection "to be punctilious in honouring acceptances", besides the facility of (premature) discounting with regard to bills exchange (which may apply even to "accommodation bills" not backed by any sale transaction as such). *Thirdly,* the concept may be further widened, so that the ratio of current assets to FEO may be described as "current interval". Here, the numerator covers (besides quick assets) other current assets also (mainly inventories, which the firm hopes to convert into cash, *either* directly through cash sales, *or via* receivables in respect of credit sales). However, this may import a great deal of uncertainty into calculations. *Fourthly,* the ratio of "defensive assets *minus* current liabilities" to FEO may be described as "no-credit interval". According to the rule-of-thumb, quick assets should be at least equal to (and not less than) current liabilities. Any excess of quick assets over current liabilities would make this ratio positive (a symptom of strength). If quick assets fall short of current liabilities, the ratio would be negative (a sign of weakness). When quick assets are just equal to current liabilities, no-credit interval would be zero. That is, nothing would be left (out of quick assets), after paying current liabilities, for meeting (day-to-day) operating expenses. A variant of this exercise could take the excess of current assets over current liabilities as the numerator.

3.5 Valuation Ratios

The word "value" is used in French as a feminine of "value"/past participle of "velour", which means "to be strong" (valour/velour standing for great courage, bravery or fearlessness). The origin of "value" or "valuation" can also be traced to the Latin word "Valera," which means about the same (to be worth/to be strong). In economics, a distinction is sought to be made between "value in use" (utility yielded by the consumption/ possession of an object/commodity) and "value in exchange" (known as "price" when expressed in money and as "goods equivalent" in the context of barter). Although both these concepts are intimately interlinked, it is the second sense which appears more relevant to "valuation ratios" which are also known as "market tests." That is, the merit or worth of a company, as judged by prospective investors/shareholders, is reflected in stock exchange quotations (or in the price which a purchaser is prepared to pay for a firm including its goodwill). In other words, "value" is a commercial/monetary index of how much a firm is prized or held in respect and admiration by the business community, governmental agencies, and the society as a whole.

Accordingly, "valuation" is the estimation of a firm's worth, or the value set upon anything, specially by-professional values. A number of valuation ratios can be thought of in this context. First, "valuation ratio" may be defined as the ratio of market value of equity capital to the book value of assets. The market value of equity shares (common stock) is guided mainly by two instincts:

investment instinct (the rate of return/amount of dividend likely to be available); and

speculative instinct (the amount of capital appreciation, or the benefit likely to flow from fluctuations in the prices of shares in the foreseeable future).

The amount of dividend is a function of the total profit available for distribution and the policy adopted by the company with regard to "retention versus payout". Too much of retention may result in a lowering down of share prices (in spite of the prospect of capital appreciation), thus making the firm vulnerable to "takeover" by other companies. If "payout" is too high, the current market price of shares may swing up, but long-term sustenance may be jeopardized (on account of the poor prospect of capital appreciation, and the difficulty in maintaining uniformly high rates of dividend). As such, top management may be forced to think of an "equilibrium rate" of dividend, and of the firm's growth.

Second, the ratio of earnings (available for distribution to equity shareholders) to equity share capital outstanding (nominal value standing in the Balance Sheet) may be worked out. The term earnings, in this context, would imply the net profit after payment of interest on debt, taxes on income, and dividend on preference capital. The remaining amount may not, necessarily, be-paid away in the form of dividend to equity shareholders. A part (or even the whole) of it may be transferred to the general reserve/reserve fund. As such, the earnings (in this context) imply the maximum amount which may be used for payment of dividend to holders of common stock (besides the possibility of using reserves built up out of profits earned in earlier accounting periods). So far as the denominator is concerned, it ignores the market price altogether.

Only the amount standing in the books under the head of equity share capital (common stock) is taken into account. If such shares are fully paid up, the "nominal/face value" and the paid-up amount would be the same. However, if these shares are partly paid up, only the amount actually paid up would be taken into account (although the nominal/face value, which is higher, could also be used as the denominator). In any case, share premium gets excluded (even though it forms part of the original investment made by equity shareholders).

To avoid these difficulties, the "number" of equity shares may be used as the denominator. In that case, the ratio may be described as "earnings per share". It may, however, be added that this would not be applicable to the term "stock" as used in India (for fully paid shares converted into a consolidated whole amount without specifying the number of shares comprising that stock certificate). Sometimes, it is also considered necessary to work out the ratio of "cash flow" to tangible assets or net worth.

Third, the ratio of "earnings per share" to "market price of equity share" may be calculated. It is known as earnings-price (E/P) ratio. The definition of earnings here is the same as given in the previous paragraph with reference to the second ratio. The market price of equity share, however, is capable of several interpretations. It may mean the closing quotation on the last day of the accounting period (for which earnings are being taken into account). Or, it may stand for the price at which the last transaction (in that share) has taken place prior to the point of time when computation (of this ratio) is being done. But such isolated indications of price per share may not be they representative of the general trend. As such, it may be more meaningful to work out an average of the price prevailing over the accounting period.

A crude method of calculating this average may be to add up the Opening price (on the first day of the accounting period) and the closing price (oh the last day of the accounting period), and then to divide the aggregate figure by two. If even this average is not reliable, the exercise may be repeated for each working day, and then an average of daily averages may be worked out. Alternatively, an average of the highest and the lowest quotations (on a particular day/during the entire accounting, period) may be computed.

The speculative element may be so prominent that an equity share fluctuates within a day, by a margin greater than its face (nominal) value. A classic example is of the Tata Steel Deferred Share prior to its conversion into ordinary shares in 1954. This scrip was the market leader for no less quarter of a century. It made greater fortunes than a share in India and possibly in any stock market of the world with a face value of Rs. 30 only it was quoted at Rs. 1,152 on June 30, 1949, in the wake Independence hesitancy and confusion.

Fourth, the ratio of "market price of equity to earnings per share" may be calculated. Known as price per earning (P/E) ratio, it is the reciprocal of E/P ratio discussed above (third ratio). For the Tata Steel Deferred Share, the P/E would be as high as: 48.5 percent in the 1946 peak and, relatively low at 15.4 percent in the 1949 trough. Both these (E/P and P/E) ratios seek to establish the performance of a company (earnings available for distribution) and the market price of its equity share.

Thus, any in the price of a share, not (fully) warranted by (change level of) earnings, is immediately reflected in these two ratios. An increase in the E/P ratio (or a decrease in the

P/E: an indication of reduced (level of) confidence on the investors (toward the company). The bank rate in India at that time was low (only 3 percent). Even then, the recovery period did not go very much beyond 33 (much lower than the high figure of 48 years). In other words, the investors/speculators had confidence in Tata Steel Deferred Shares (with an E/P of just 21 percent in 1946) than in Government Paper (available at par with interest around 3 percent per annum).

Such faith could emanate from the quality of management (as revealed by expansion/modernization plans, product improvement/diversification, stable/growing market share, harmonious industrial relations, and other qualitative dimensions). People had tremendous faith in the integrity, innovative character and other leadership qualities of Mr. J.R.D. Tata who having taken over as Chairman of Tata Iron and Steel Company in 1938, continued in that position for a record 46 years (up to 1984).

No other concern of such dimension in India (and possibly, in other countries also) witnessed so much of unpunctuated industrial peace over this half century (which encompassed the Second World War and many other tumultuous events). However, the high water-mark of P/E ratio, and the magnitude of fluctuations therein, had also been indicative of a massive "speculation spiral" which culminated in the conversion of TISCO's deferred shares into ordinary shares in 1954, and in the elimination of the third tier (deferred/management/founders' shares) below the two tiers (preference and ordinary shares), which only remained permissible in India under the Companies Act of 1956.

Fifth, the ratio of dividend (amount per share) to paid-up value of share may be computed. This is called the dividend rate (percent). Here the numerator is actual dividend per share, and not the earnings (available for distribution) per share as in case of E/P (third) ratio. Further, the denominator is the actual amount paid on a share, and not its market price as with E/P ratio. In the case of partly paid-up shares, the denominator would be different from (less than) the nominal/face value of a share. The quotient is multiplied by 100, since this ratio (dividend rate, like the E/P and P/E ratios), is usually expressed as a percentage. In the case of Tata Steel Deferred Share referred to in the last two paragraphs, the dividend rate was as high as 250 percent (on the assumption that the sum of Rs. 75 was dividend per share, which was fully paid in respect of its face value appearing at Rs. 30).

Sixth, the ratio of market price per share to its face value (nominal value, or paid-up value in respect of a share which is not fully paid up) may be worked out. This is known as the "share price index" usually expressed as a percentage). An index of less than 100 (which is something like a "benchmark") is a symptom of poor (bad) rating on the part of stock market (investors/speculators). With the index standing at 100, the rating is deemed to be indifferent. When the share pries index advances beyond 100, it is an evidence of good rating (which may become better and better if this advance continues).

However, this rating is not, necessarily, based on the micro-economic performance of a firm. Macro-economic expectations, emerging from the overall socio-political environment, techno-managerial change, and governmental policies (fiscal/monetary/commercial/industrial) have much to do with the market rating of shares. And the activities of speculators have their own role in widening the extremities of "bullish" and "bearish" situations. That is, the "psychology of boom" pushes up the price index still further, whereas an "apprehension of crash" hastens its downward movement.

Thus, in the case of Tata Steel Deferred Share, discussed in connection with E/P and P/E ratios, the share price index rose from 4,400 in 1939 to 12,100 in 1946. In general, the Second World War contributed substantially to this boom. However, during this period, the market confidence got suddenly shattered in the wake of Calcutta's bombardment (1943), which led to the paralysation of stock exchange activity for a couple of months. More recently, high-level expectations regarding economic liberalization and modernization, under Mr. Rajiv Gandhi's government in India, ushered in an unusual stock market boom after the presentation of the Union budget for the fiscal year 1985-86.

Seventh, the ratio of dividend (amount per share) to "market price of share" may be worked out. It is known as "yield (percent)". This relationship can also be expressed as the ratio of dividend rate (fifth ratio) to share price index (sixth ratio). In respect of Tata Steel Deferred Share, referred to above, the dividend rate was 250 percent, whereas the share price index was 12,100 in 1946. So, the yield would work out to 2.1 percent. This is also the E/P ratio, since the amount of dividend has been taken to be equivalent to earnings (available for distribution). The same result can be obtained when 75 is divided by 3,640 and the quotient is multiplied by 100.

Eighth, the ratio of total dividends (or dividend per share) to net profit after tax (or earnings per share available for distribution) may be worked out. This is known as "dividend-payout ratio", or mercy "payout ratio." If the E/P ratio (third ratio) and yield (seventh ratio) are the same, the payout ratio (eighth ratio) would be unity (or 100 percent). Alternatively, it may be said that the eighth ratio presents a combined picture of second and fifth ratios. The extent to which the payout ratio is less than unity (100 percent) could be interpreted as a measure of conservatism practiced by the relevant company in framing its dividend policy. While conservation of profits in the form of general reserve/reserve fund may, as well, add to the long-term financial strength of a firm, many shareholders have a short-term focus on the maximization of current dividend. As such, a low payout ratio may be responsible for a lowering down of the share price index.

Ninth, the ratio of retained profit to net profit after tax (available for distribution in the form of dividend) may be calculated. This is known as "profit-retention ratio" or merely "retention ratio". It is complementary to the earlier (eighth) ratio. If the payout ratio is unity (100 percent), the retention ratio would be zero. At the other extreme, if the payout ratio is zero, the retention ratio would be unity (100 percent). In between these extremes, there may be numerous alternatives, such as a payout ratio of 80 percent, along with a retention ratio of 20 percent.

Normally, the payout ratio cannot exceed 100 percent (unless past reserves are used for payment of current dividend). But if it does, the retention ratio would be a negative figure (indicating dissipation of past profits held as reserves). By definition, the retention ratio cannot exceed 100 percent (since the amount of profit retained in a particular period cannot be more than the total profit for the relevant accounting period).

As such, the payout ratio cannot be a negative figure. At this stage, it may be pertinent to introduce a brief case study of GEC (General Electric Company of India Limited) incorporated in 1911. Table 3.5 goes to indicate, respectively, its financial performance and share performance between 1980 and 1985 (October-end).

Thus, there was no necessary correspondence between financial performance and share performance of GEC, particularly during the last two years of the period under study when, the margin between "high" and "low" price quotations in the stock market suddenly widened, while the gross dividend per equity share remained constant.

The GEC equity (Rs. 10 paid up)-fluctuated around Rs. 38 during January-March 1985. After the Government of India had announced their budget proposals for 1985-86, along with some forerunners of a long-term fiscal/industrial policy (such as abolition of CDS/estate duty, reduction in the marginal rate of income tax/wealth tax, and raising the asset limit for units/groups requiring registration under Chapter II of MRTP Act from Rs. 200 million to Rs. 1,000 million), the market price of GEC equity share jumped up to Rs. 74 in August 1985 (about twice the level obtaining six months earlier).

By October 1985, it had slipped down to a "level of Rs. 52 (roughly 50 percent above the level obtaining in the first quarter of 1985). It may be noted that the rate of dividend on GEC equity share (with Rs. 10 paid up as base) was as low as 15 percent for three of the five accounting years under reference. For the remaining two years (not relevant to the 1985 boom), the dividend rate was 18 percent and 21 percent (the maximum attained over the quinqennium) respectively. These rates of dividend on equity shares of a company, belonging to an internationally renowned complex like GEC, were rather poor, particularly in the context of high rates of interest prevailing about this time (some 18 percent on commercial bank lending, 14 percent on public deposits with companies, and 11 percent on fixed deposits with scheduled banks). As such, there was little justification of the share price index rising very much beyond 100, whereas it never fell below 171 (1980) and the same went up as high as 740 (1985). The lowest quotation in 1985 (up to October-end) was more than twice the lowest figure obtaining in 1980, whereas the highest quotation of 1985 was more than thrice the highest quotation of 1980, even though the rates of dividend for the relevant accounting years did not warrant any such upswing. Some of the relevant ratios have been worked out in Table 3.5.

The denominator for E/P ratio, as also for yield (percent), has been taken to be the average share price index which works out at 252.5 for 1981, 290.5 for 1982, 346.5 for 1983, 342.5 for 1984, and 532.0 for 1985. The E/P ratio, which multiplied by the payout ratio (and then divided by 100), gives the yield (percent). By definition, the payout ratio and the retention ratio add up to 100 percent for each one of these accounting years (ending on March 31, as against share price indicates which are for each one of the calendar years ending on the following December 31, except 1985 treated at October-end).

It is surprising that stock market transactions were taking place at an yield rate as low as 2.8 percent on the average share prices index for 1985 (just 2.0 percent on the basis of the maximum price of GEC equity share quoted in August 1985, when interest rate on fixed deposits for five years was 11 percent). At the end of March 1985, total capital employed stood at Rs. 575 million, equity capital at Rs. 72 million, reserves and surplus at Rs. 146 million, loans at Rs. 65 million, accumulated depreciation at Rs. 66 million, and gross block at Rs. 115 million. Thus, with equity share capital standing at only one-eighth of total capital employed, the company would appear to have indulged in "trading on equity". In 1985, the pre-tax profits had a ratio as high as 70 percent of equity share capital, though the earnings (available for distribution to equity shareholders) were less than 30 percent, while the rate of dividend was very much lower, at 15 percent.

Table 3.5: Valuation Ratios of GEC (India)

Year	E/P Ratio	Yield Ratio	Payout	Retention
	(percent)	(percent)	Ratio	Ratio
			(percent)	(percent)
1981	12.4	5.9	48.1	51.9
1982	15.3	6.2	40.5	59.5
1983	12.0	6.1	50.5	'49.5
1984	6.9	4.4	63.8	36.2
1985	5.6	2.8	50.0	50.0

Thus, even trading on equity cannot be said to have yielded much except for the benefits of capital appreciation, which was largely psychic, having been actually reaped by only a few of the older shareholders. So far as speculators are concerned, the gains going to some might have been counterbalanced by the losses loaded on certain others.

A high retention ratio can be said to have imparted internal financial strength to the company whose accumulated reserves and surplus had a ratio of 203 percent to equity share capital (as the denominator). To a smaller extent, this may also be true of accumulated depreciation, which had a ratio of 57 percent to gross block.

Another (though hidden) source of strength appeared to be the substantial support drawn from trade creditors for financing gross working capital (current assets). It is significant to note that interest-bearing loans were not on the high side (being actually less than equity share capital), whereas gross block was only 20 percent of total capital employed.

The ratio of sales to capital employed, too, appeared to be quite favourable at 126 percent for 1985. However, the ratio of pre-tax profit to sales was quite low at 7.5 percent. Multiplying these to secondary ratios (and then dividing the-product by 100), the primary ratio of net profit to capital employed, or return on investment (RO1) is found to be slightly better at 9.4 percent. Yet, the overall profitability ratio was, undoubtedly, poor.

The market value of equity shares in 1985 was much too high in relation thereto. But, in spite of this boom, the overall valuation ratio (the ratio of the market value of equity capital to the book value of assets/capital employed) would appear to be somewhat low at 0.67 on the basis of average share price and 0.90 on the basis of maximum share price in 1985. That is in either case, it was less than the benchmark of unity (1.00).

Tenth, the ratio of retained profit to total assets (total liabilities) or tangible assets (capital employed) may be calculated. In the GEC case referred to above, this ratio works out at 25 percent, which is fairly high. It means that one-fourth of the undertaking (tangible assets/capital employed) has been built up with the owners' savings (profits withheld from distribution and ploughed back into the undertaking) belonging to equity shareholders.

It augurs well for the company's solvency so that, even if the tangible assets depreciate (get eroded) to the extent of 25 percent, the firm can still meet, in full, all its formal obligations (including repayment of equity share capital in the event of liquidation). This also lends strength to the company's profitability inasmuch as one-fourth of the capital employed carries no annual obligation (whether in the form of interest or dividend) repayment burden, while there is the positive possibility of using past profits for maintaining stable rate of dividend in lean year(s).

Eleventh, the ratio of "net liquidation value" to equity share capital may be computed. The numerator is ascertained by adding up the expected liquidation values of all the assets, and then deducting there from the anticipated liquidation values of all kinds of debt (which may include preference share capital also).

A rough-and-ready measure of valuation, propounded by Wilcox goes to suggest that the liquidation value is 100 percent for cash equivalents, 70 percent for other current assets, 50 percent for long-term assets, and 100 percent for debt. Wilcox assumes that the change in "financial state" (caused from year to year by inflows and outflows) always takes place by a fixed amount (symbolized as *S,* or "size of the bet"). If the probability of the firm's gaining the bet is and that of" losing the bet is q, the firm is bound to fail unless exceeds q.

This is a rather arbitrary method of judging the reserve strength of a company. The higher the ratio of net liquidation value (adjusted cash position) to the paid-up amount of equity shares, the better would a company be able to fulfil the market test (that is, the greater would be the justification for the market price of its shares to rise).

Strictly speaking, if this ratio is unity (100 percent), the company's equity share should be quoted at par (that is, the share price index should be 100). Accordingly, if the ratio is 125 percent, the price index should be 125, and, when the ratio is 75 percent, the price index should be 75 (that is, below par). This ratio puts its main focus on the solvency of a company, so that the level of profitability (except, in as far as its may affect solvency indirectly) gets ignored.

Twelfth, the ratio of "retained profit *plus* depreciation charge" to debt may be calculated. This ratio puts its focus on profitability (in a cumulative sense), though not in relation to the valuation of equity shares *directly*. However, in an indirect sense, it serves as a market test. If this ratio is greater than unity (more than 100 percent), there may be justification for equity shares to be sold above par (that is, for the share price index to rise beyond 100). A variant of this relationship may be arrived at (after excluding depreciation charge from the numerator) by computing the "pure" ratio of retained profit to debt. Such a ratio may also have some use for adjudging the fair market value of creditor ship securities (bonds/ debentures), specially when these are sought to be converted into ownership stock (equity share capital).

Thirteenth, the ratio of *actual* earnings (available for distribution to equity shareholders) to *normally, expected* level of earnings may be worked out. This may be called as "(income) capitalization value (index)", serving to indicate the fair market value of an equity share (with 100 as base). For example, in the GEC case referred to above, the actual earnings per share for 1985 figured at Rs. 2.98.

If the expected level (norm) was Rs. 2.00 (20 percent on a paid-up value of Rs. 10) per share, the index of capitalization value would be 149, so that an equity share of Rs. 10 could be quoted at Rs. 14.90. However, then the lowest price in 1985 (up to October-end) was more than twice this figure, whereas the maximum price ruling in August 1985 was nearly five times this "fair quotation".

It may of course be noted that the index of capitalization value puts the entire focus on current earnings, so that the solvency aspect (even in the context of retained earnings) gets eclipsed.

Moreover, it may not be easy to determine a norm of earnings which may hold valid for a fairly long period encompassing both macro-level and micro-level changes. However, a firm may prepare "stability of earnings index"

index (normalization measure based on standard' deviation/error in respect of return assets, say, over a ten-year period. Such micro-exercises may be followed by macro-computations for the "industry rage" or "area average," the reliability of which may depend the extent to which the subnormal performance of certain is evenly balanced by the supernormal performance of other firms in that group. In other words, the universe has to fairly large, uniform (in respect of size, technology, product etc.) and competitive ("non-monopolistic) in character.

The presentation of a truly comparative picture, in any case, would have an element of time lag which may be crucial for the market (and even in the application of market tests to other situations. A quick recipe would be to use the prevailing rate of interest (paid by commercial banks on, say, five-year fixed deposits, or the interest charged by such banks/other financial institutions on loans granted/bills discounted, or the bank rate charged by the central bank of a country on bills of exchange rediscounted) as a guideline.

For example, the rate of expected earnings on equity earnings may be placed at, say, 5 percent above the fixed deposit rate (11 percent *plus 5* percent= J6 percent), or 2 percent above the commercial lending rate (say, 18 percent *plus 2* percent=20 percent). Easier still may be to accept the relevant rate of interest (itself) has the basic norm without any moderation/modification. Alternatively, a "weighted capitalization rate" may be worked out after taking into account the capital structure of a company. Table 3.6 may serve to illustrate this point.

Fourteenth, the ratio of supernormal profit (or super profit) to retained earnings may be calculated. Such a ratio is based on the implicit assumption that the normal investment (capital structure) of a firm is able to yield normal profit (expected rate of earnings as interpreted in the previous paragraph), so that profits ploughed back (retained earnings reinvested) must yield super-profit (over and above normal profit) at a rate which is not lower than the expected level of earnings. Thus, if the ratio of super-profit to retained earnings is 34 percent, and the norm of earnings stands prescribed at 17 percent, there may be justification for the share price index to rise up to 200. That is, an equity share with a. paid-up value of Rs. 10 may be quoted at Rs. 20 in the stock market. Such a relationship, in a way, is an attempt to build a bridge between solvency and profitability, with an integrated focus on market valuation.

Table 3.6: Weighted Capitalization Rate

Capital component	Proportion of total capita! (percent)	Applicable rate (percent)	Weighted cost (percent) 1
Debt	40	15	6
Preference Cap	25	16	1
Equity Capital	35 •	20	7
Total	100	17	17

This ratio may be quite meaningful for a firm financed exclusively or principally by its owners. That is, a company which has relied substantially on preference share capital, debentures/bonds, public deposits and other borrowings, may not be able to identify a *straight* relationship between super-profit and retained earnings (in the context of a complicated capital structure).

Again, this ratio may not be relevant to companies following liberal dividend policies, so that little profit is available for reinvestment. In the GEC case referred to above, retained, profit was quite large (more than twice the amount paid up on equity shares). With 17 percent as the expected norm of earnings, the total earnings per share should have been 52 percent, so as to leave a super-profit of 35 percent on equity share capital (or 17 percent on retained profit). But the actual earnings were less than 30 percent (Rs. 2.98, on Rs. 10 paid-up share), so that super-profit was less than 13 percent on equity share capital (or some 6 percent on retained profit).

According to this criterion, the GEC equity share should have been quoted at much below par in 1985. However, if pre-tax profit (Rs. 54 million) is taken into account, its ratio to equity capital (Rs. 72 million) would be as high as 75 percent, so that, after allowing for a normal profit of 17 percent (about Rs. 12 million), a super-profit of Rs. 42 million would be available.

The ratio of this super-profit to retained earnings (Rs. 146 million) would be about 29 percent so that the fair market value of a GEC equity share (Rs. 10 paid up) would be Rs. 17 (less than one-fourth of the "high" and about half of the "low") in 1985. Incidentally, the rate of pre-tax profit on retained earnings (29 percent) is about the same as the earnings (available for distribution) per share (29.80 percent). The ratio of pre-tax profit to "equity share capital *plus* retained earnings" works out to about 25 percent.

A variant of the above-mentioned relationship (ratio of super-profit to retained earnings) may be the ratio of super-profit to gross *real* investment (additions to inventory and fixed assets). Presuming that normal profit was earned in the year on the *real* capital stock (inventory and fixed assets) the existing, this ratio, in effect, measures the relationship between incremental profit and incremental *real* capital stock. So to say it verges on (incremental) output-capital (or, capital-output ratio which is proposed to be examined later on, at some length in this volume.

Another variant of this relationship may be the ratio of super-profit to the "appropriate rate for capitalization of super-profit". The denominator can be the same rate (return) beyond which profit is deemed to be super-profit. For example, it may be taken to be 17 percent as indicated in the GEC case referred to above, or the prevailing rate of interest (say 11 percent on five-year fixed deposits), or any other (higher/lower) rate deemed appropriate.

The capitalization value so arrived at (after dividing the super-profit by capitalization rate, and then multiplying the quotient by 10 represents the goodwill or premium which (equity) shareholder can appropriate to themselves in the context of market valuation. Thus, the total value of a business may be arrived at adding this (additional) capitalization value to the value of n tangible assets.

If the numerator were taken to be the tot profit (instead of super-profit only), one could (directly) arrive at the (total) capitalization value which, itself, would represent the value of that business (so that the amount of goodwill or premium on shares could be ascertained by deducting the value of net tangible assets from that capitalization value). If the actual rate of earnings is less than the normal annual rate (return appropriate to the business), the total capitalization value would fall short of the value of net tangible assets and the additional capitalization value representing goodwill would be a negative figure.

In such a situation, the fair market valuation of an equity share would appear below its par (paid up) value. The following equation can be used to illustrate the ratio of super-profit to the appropriate capitalization rate for assessing the total value of a business and the premium which its owners can hope to avail of in the stock market, where:

V represents the total value of a-business to-be ascertained;

A represents the value of net tangible assets in that business;

P represents actual (or anticipated) earnings in that business;

R represents the normal actual rate of return appropriate to the business (capitalization rate);

P—rA represents the super-profit;

J represents the appropriate rate for capitalization of the super-profit (which rate can be the same as, or different from, r referred to above); and

P—rA represents the value of goodwill or premium available

J to the owners of that business (equity shareholders).

Fifteenth, the ratio of "total market value of stock (equity)" to "total market value of the firm" (or net worth to total assets) may be worked out. A complementary ratio of "total market value of bonds (debt)" to "total market value of the firm" may also be computed.

These ratios may be based on the assumption that *V* (total market value of the *firm)=S* (total market value of stock)+B (total market value of bonds). As such, these two ratios would add up to one (or 100 percent). In consequence, it may be suggested that 5= *V— B.* On this score, David Durand identified the two extreme cases in a key article quoted by Weston and Brigham:

> **Net Income Approach (NI):** Under the NI approach to valuation, the interest rate and the cost of capital are independent of the capital structure, but the weighted average or overall cost of capital declines, and the total value (value of stock *plus* value of debt) rises, with increased use of leverage.
>
> **Net Operating Income Approach (NOT):** Under the NOI approach, the cost of equity increases, the weighted average cost of capital remains constant, and the total value *of the* firm also remains constant as leverage is changed.

Franco Modigliani (winner of Nobel Prize in Economics for 1985) and Merton Miller (MM) strongly supported NOI in their several publications, viz.:

> "The Cost of Capital, Corporation Finance and the Theory of Investment" *(American Economic Review,* June 1958);
>
> "The Cost of Capital, Corporation Finance and the Theory of Investment: Reply" *(American Economic Review,* September 1958);
>
> "Taxes and the Cost of 'Capital: A .Correction" *(American Economic Review,* June 1963); and
>
> "Reply" *(American Economic Review,* June 1965).

In their original hypothesis, MM (Modigliani and Miller)

assumed that:

personal (homemade) (leverage and corporate leverage are perfect substitutes in the context of arbitrage process (sales of the levered firm's stock pushing its price down, and purchases of the unlevered firm's stock driving its prices up),

there are no transaction costs in this process.

corporations and individuals borrow at the same rate,

there are no institutional restrictions which may retard the arbitrage process, and

there are no taxes.

MM argued that the NI approach, creating a wedge between *U* (unlevered firm) and *L* (levered firm), as symbolized by the following table, cannot persist for long (since the arbitrage process would continue until the market values of the two firms are equal).

The value of common stock (equity share has been assessed with a capitalization rate/cost of capital (k_s) of 20 percent, whereas for debt (bonds/debentures), the capitalization rate/cost of capital (k_b) has been taken at 15 percent (the rate at which the levered firm is obliged to pay interest).

The element of taxation has been ignored. The net operating income (EBIT=earnings before interest and taxes) is the same for both the firms. By implication, the total investment (the paid-up value of stock *plus* debt) is also the same (Rs. 300 million). There is, however, difference in capital structure. Firm *U* has common stock with a paid-up value of Rs 300 million (whose market value is only Rs. 276 million), whereas firm *L* has common stock with a paid-up value of Rs, 200 million *plus* debt figuring at Rs. 100 million (the total market value thus amounting to Rs. 300 million).

Equity shareholders in firm *L* ,are just able to get 20 percent dividend on their paid-up value (which is also their market value in this case), while those in firm *U* can get a dividend of a little over 18 percent on paid-up value (which works out to just 20 percent on their below-par market value). As such, the original subscribers to common stock in firm *U* may feel disadvantaged at this juncture. But the holders of common stock in firm *L* may be standing at the end of a more dangerous precipice.

If, due to recession, there is decline in EBIT from Rs. 55 million to Rs. 30 million, the amount available for dividend on firm L's common stock would fall to 7.5 percent, whereas firm *U* could pay dividend at a higher rate of 10 percent to holders of its common stock. With a further fall in EBIT to Rs. 6 million, firm *U* might still pay a dividend of 2 percent, whereas *E* in firm *L* turns into a negative figure (so that the bulk of interest on debt has to be met out of owner's equity). In the context of this vulnerability, it has been argued by MM that there may be pressure on holders of common stock (and maybe even bonds) in firm *L* to unload their holdings, leading to a depression in its total market value.

On the contrary, there may be a buying spree in respect of the common stock of firm *U*, leading to an appreciation in its market value. According to MM, these arbitrage dealings would bring about an equalization in the total market value of the two (unleveled and levered) firms.

In fine, the MM hypothesis suggests that capital structure is irrelevant to the overall market valuation of a firm, a proposition which can draw considerable support from theory, but which may appear to have been drawn a little 100 far from reality (stock market situations discussed earlier).

The Modigliani-Miller (MM) view, in its "corrected" form, concedes that (when taxes are taken into account), a levered firm commands a higher value because interest on debt is a deductible expense. According to MM, the value of firm *L* exceeds that of firm *U* by an amount equal to L's debt multiplied by the tax rate. Reduced to an equation, $Vi = V_n + Bt$ (where V_t — value of firm *L*, F=value of firm *U*, *B*=amount of debt in L, and *t*-=tax rate). With a tax rate of 40 percent, the profit after tax (PAT) would be Rs. 33 million for firm *U* and

Rs. 24 million for firm L.

As such, the former can pay Rs. 33 million only to suppliers of (long-term) capital, whereas the latter can pay Rs. 39 million (Rs. 24 million by way of dividend, over and above Rs. 15 million in the form of interest), that is Rs. 7 million more (to holders of common stock .and bonds put together). So, according to the *corrected* MM hypothesis, the total market value of firm *L* would be higher than that of *U* by this margin, which is the saving in taxation (Rs. 22 million *minus* Rs. 16 million).

This amount of Rs. 6 million *(Bt)* can be arrived at, in terms of the equation, after multiplying the amount of debt (Rs. 15 million) by the rate of tax (40 percent).

The cost of retained earnings *(kr)* can also be worked out in terms of "before tax" and "after tax" required rate of return. Nantell and Carlson define it 'as that rate of return which the firm must earn on projects financed by retained earnings in order to keep stockholders at least as well oft' in terms of their wealth as if the firm had paid the earnings out as dividends.

This can be visualized as an appropriate cut-off rate for investment decisions; and the same may have to be computed as a weighted average of each of the component costs, in case the financial policy of the firm involves other sources of funds in addition to retained earnings. That is, *kr* is that rate of return which a firm must earn on the funds retained so as to equate the "with retention" price of the common stock (equity shares) to the market price prevailing when (if) the funds are not retained.

This can be judged in terms of the "super profit" concept already examined under the fourteenth ratio. Here, reference may be made to two other approaches: *first* as an alternative to payment of dividend; and, *secondly,* as an alter- native to the firm purchasing its own stock (if permissible) or the stock of comparable companies (or making any other investment outside the firm). The first approach may call for the- consideration of various factors, such as:

the rate of tax on dividends,

the rate of tax on retained earnings,

the rate of corporation tax on company profits,

the rate of personal income tax applicable to dividends received by stockholders,

the rate of capital gains tax applicable to appreciation in the value of stock,

rates of wealth tax and other direct taxes/impositions (including excess profits tax, surtax, surcharges, etc.) having their impact on the divisible profits of a firm and/or on the net income available to the owners.

While adopting the second approach, the factors to be taken into account may include:

the prevailing rates of interest available on time deposits (as also on demand deposits, if any),

the market price of the common stock (equity shares) of that company,

the prevailing prices of the shares of comparable companies,

the rates of dividend/payout ratios/financial policies (including issue of bonus shares/rights shares/convertible debentures/redeemable preference shares, etc.),

prevailing restrictions on share transfers, and (vi) cost/time involved in effecting such transfers.

Besides, there may be other administrative costs and procedural constraints relevant to both the approaches referred to here. But, (above all, there may be the *hidden factor* (relevant to both these approaches) regarding the psychology of those who buy, retain and sell company shares.

This "psychological ratio" would indicate the extent to which retained earnings can be a substitute for dividends (so that the market valuation of shared remains undisturbed). It may be more meaningful to view this as an *incremental ratio.*

For example, an equity share of the face value of Rs. 100 is selling at par and receiving a dividend of 15 percent (equal to what is available on bonds). Now, if the psychological ratio is 1.5 (with the choice of retained earnings as numerator and the choice of additional dividend as denominator), the company must retain 9 percent to compensate for (the absence of) an additional dividend of 6 percent, in order to have an identical market valuation (say at Rs. 140 per share).

Such a ratio may, as well, be relevant to a choice between. The issue of bonus shares and the payment of cash dividend, or to a comparison of the "payout *versus* retention policies" two similar firms. In the latter situation, the firm which opts in favour of reception must be capable of earning incremental profit (beyond the basic rate, say 15 percent) to a rate 50 percent more than the other firm which goes in for the (obviously softer) option of paying additional dividend.

This may be interpreted as some kind of liquidity, preference/discounting of future emanating from a typically short-term outlook even of long-term investors. It is like the traditional psychology of maximizing today's milk output unmindful of the adverse impact on the health of the calf and on tomorrow's milk-yielding capacity of the milk cow.

To counteract this skimming psychology, the government could impose a tax on (additional) dividend (say, at the rate of 50 percent). A somewhat similar tax could be imposed on the issue of bonus shares(which may represent a halfway house between "total retention" and "cash payment of dividend" if the government wishes to guard against the possible decline share prices consequent upon the widening of dividend–sharing "capital base".

That is (besides legal restrictions obtaining in India and other countries), bonus shares additional share capital may (justifiably) be issued only by those companies whose marginal efficiency of capital is high enough to meet the normal expectation of growth in dividends on the total (erstwhile/new) capital stock. The following simple equations may be useful in indicating the likely impact of bonus/rights issue on the market valuation of relevant shares.

(A) Issue of bonus shares

$$P2 = \frac{H1 \times P1}{H1 + H2}$$

where,

P2 is the ex-bonus market price per share to be ascertained.

H1 is the existing holding of shares (say 1000).

H2 is the (proposed) addition, to existing holding of shares, in the form of bonus shares (say 200).

P1 is the existing (pre-bonus) market price per share, say Rs. 132 for a share of the face value of Rs. 100).

then,

$$P2 = \frac{1000 \times 132}{1000 + 200} = \frac{132000}{1200}$$

=Rs. 110

Issue of rights shares for cash

$$P3 = \frac{(H1 \times P1) + (H2 \times P2)}{H1 + H2}$$

where,

P3 is the ex-rights price (per share) to be ascertained.

H1 is the existing holding of shares (say 1000).

H2 is the (proposed) addition to existing share holding in the form of rights shares, say 200).

P1 is the cum-rights price per share (say Rs. 132 for as share of the face value of Rs. 1000 prevailing before the issue of the rights share).

P2 is the concessional price over share, say Rs. 1200 at which rights shares are offered (rights price).

then,

$$P3 = \frac{(1000 \times 132) + (200 \times 120)}{1000 + 200}$$

$$= \frac{156000}{1200} = \text{Rs. } 130$$

and,

VRS (value of right per share)

$$= \frac{H2(P1 - P2)}{H1 + H2}$$

$$= \frac{200\,(132-120)}{1000+200}$$

$$= \frac{2400}{1200} = \text{Rs. } 2$$

Alternatively,

VRS = P1-P3=132-130

= Rs. 2

Sixteenth, the ratio of the value of an amalgamated firm to the aggregate value of separate firms may be worked relationship can be used as a test of the desirability (commercial viability) of a (proposed) amalgamation merger of two or more firms operating independently. Here, the benchmark is unity. When the synergy ratio stands at this level, it is interpreted to mean that the process of amalgamation is neutral in terms of valuation. That is, status quo is maintained, in as much as the value of the combined firm is just equal to the sum total of the value of aggregated firms.

With SR>1, there is case for amalgamation, while these is no such justification (on the basis of valuation criterion) if SR<1. The "synergetic effect"(SE) is measured by the extent to which SR is greater than unity (SR minus 1) if SR is less than unity, SE will be a negative figure. For example, X and Y are two separate firms with a valuation of Rs. 180,000 (1,000 shares of the face value of Rs. 100 valued at Rs. 180 each) and Rs. 120,000 (500 shares of the face value of Rs. 100, valued at Rs. 240 each). Now, X and Y can combine in a number of ways so as to have complete integration.

Either one firm (say Y) gets merged into another firm (say X), or a new firm (say Y) gets merged into another firm (say X), or a new firm (say "XY" or "Z") is constituted to take over both X and Y for the purpose of equations to follow, the amalgamated firm will be called Z, whether, formally, it is known as (new) "X" or "XY". The following situations may be visualized to illustrate the varying levels or SR and SE.

It may be added that "size" is an important variable or

valuing the status of an organization, whether it is, or it is not, a case of "synergy". As such it may be relevant to calculate the following ratios (inter alia) to focus attention on the growth and size of firms:

(a) Annual percentage (simple or compound) growth in the size of assets of the same firm over a number of years;
(b) Ratios of the asset values of various firms at various points of time;
(c) Comparative growth rates in respect of the size of assets of several firms (or several divisional/subsidiaries of a multi-plant/multinational holding company) over a number of years;
(d) Separate breakdown of the ratios, referred to under (a) to (c), on the basis of fixed and current assets separately, as also the ratios worked out on the basis of other criteria of size, such as sales turnover and profit/earnings;
(e) Size of assets as a proportion of national income (GNP or NNP), which may be relevant to giant corporation like those appearing in the Fortune's international list;
(f) Comparative percentage changes in the "size of assets" and the price level" (general or specific for various assets in the process of revaluation/inflation accounting), so as to reflect on the "net increase" in the size of assets.

Seventeenth, a number of other relationships, with their particular focus on retained profit/depreciation charge, can be worked out. Some of these ratios are given below:

(a) Ratio of "retained profit plus depreciation charge" to "tangible assets plus accumulated depreciation";
(b) Ratios of retained profit minus (a proportion of) additions during the year to trade debtors and inventory" to total tangible assets;
(c) Ratios of "retained profit plus depreciation charge minus (a proportion of) additions during the year to trade debtors and inventory" to total tangible assets;
(d) Ratio of depreciation charge to sales (net of excise);
(e) Ratio of depreciation charge to net fixed assets; and

(f) Ratio of depreciation charge to gross fixed assets.

3.6 Summary

Liquidity is the ease with which an asset can be exchanged for money. It tends to be a matter of degree (relative concept). Not one liquidity ratio, but several such ratios may be worked out. The following is an illustrative (and not exhaustive) list (here, as elsewhere, the readers are advised to see numerous variants and other connected ratios in the text):

1. Current ratio (current assets to current liabilities);
2. Quick acid test ratio (quick or defensive assets to current liabilities);
3. Ratio of net working capital to inventory;
4. Ratio of net working capital to receivables;
5. Ratio of short-term loans to working capital gap;
6. Ratio of short-term loans to gross working capital;
7. Ratio of net working capital to all long-term funds;
8. Ratio of net working capital to tangible assets (or total assets);
9. Ratio of current liabilities (short-term debt) to tangible assets;
10. Ratio of trade creditors to inventories (or ratio of "short term bank borrowing minus cash and bank balance" to "inventories plus trade debtors");
11. Ratio of cash current assets (working capital) or quick assets to fixed assets (or total assets)
12. Ratio of cash to total assets (or tangible assets);
13. Ratio of cash or "variability or liquidity to current assets (or current liabilities);
14. Ratio of receivables to current assets (or current liabilities);
15. Ratio of inventories to current assets(or current liabilities);
16. Ratio of quick assets to current assets (or total/tangible assets) and ratio of quick assets to inventories;
17. Ratio of quick assets to inventories.

For a business, sales represent the main plank of activity

("turnover" indicating the completion of a business process or cycle of activity, represented by sales). The following (inter alia) activity/turnover ratios may be worked out:

1. Ratio of turnover to inventories (cost of goods sold to stock-in-trade);
2. Ratio of receivables (trade debtors) to 9credit sales) turnover (debtors ratio);
3. Ratio of payables to credit purchases (creditors ratio);
4. Ratio of turnover to gross working capital (current assets);
5. Ratio of turnover to net working capital (also "sales to cash" and "sales to quick assets");
6. Ratio of turnover to fixed assets;
7. Ratio of turnover to total assets (or tangible assets or net worth);
8. Ratio of turnover to the excess of receivable over payables;
9. Super ratio of average payment period to average collection period (terms of trade ratio);
10. Ratio of "receivables plus advances to suppliers" to turnover;
11. Ratio of turnover to " inventories plus advances to suppliers";
12. Ratio of payables to turnover;
13. Ratio of current liabilities to turnover;
14. Ratio of turnover to capital employed (or net worth);
15. Ageing ratios of receivables;
16. Ageing ratios of payables; and
17. Ageing ratios (super ratios) of payables and receivables;

Solvency implies ability to "pay all one's debts" (both long term and short term obligations). It is sometimes termed as "long run liquidity". The term "leverage" implies the choice (manipulation) of an appropriate capital structure/capital gearing/debt ratio, so as to ensure appropriate " coverage" of (fixed) annual obligations by the level of earnings and that of debt by owners' fund (as a determinal of the prospect of replacement). The following are some of the solvency/leverage ratios:

1. ratio of debt to equity (total debt or outside/liabilities to net worth) or " equity-total capital ratio";
2. ratio of long-term debt to net worth/equity;
3. ratio of long-term debt to permanent capital;
4. ratio of long term debt to total liabilities (total assets or tangible assets);
5. ratio of (total) debt to tangible assets (or total debt to total assets)
6. ratio of fixed assets (net block) to net worth (F/W) ratio);
7. ratio of capital employed to liabilities (proprietors' earned);
8. ratio of debt servicing to annual fund;
9. ratio of "total debt (short term and long term) plus (redeemable) preference share capital" to annual fund;
10. ratio of "total debt (with or without preference capital) to operating cash flow" (OFC) or "cash flow" (CF);
11. ratio of long term debt to net working capital;
12. ratio of all bank borrowings (current liabilities) to talk assets;
13. ratio of all bank borrowings to sales;
14. ratio of interest (with or without amortization) to sales (gross or net of excise);
15. ratio of net fixed assets to gross fixed assets; and
16. ratio of current liabilities to net worth.

Profit is an index of proficiency or progress as typified by the gain in excess of revenue over expenditure, resulting from the employment of capital (and/or risk-taking) in any transaction/activity. Profitability is the capacity of an organization/activity to earn profits in the normal course of operation. The following profitability ratios may be worked out:

1. Ratio of gross operating profit to sales (gross operating margin;
2. Ratio of "cost of goods sold(cost of sales/direct costs)" to sales;

3. Ratio of (net) operating profit to sales (ratio of "net profit" or cash flow to sales or "net sales");
4. Ratio of depreciation to sales;
5. Ratio of indirect expenses to sales;
6. Ratio of "cost of goods sold plus operating expenses" to sales;
7. Ratio of profit before tax (PBT) to sales;
8. Ratio of interest (net) to sales;
9. Ratio of profit after tax (PAT) to sales;
10. Ratio of tax to sales s9as also "assets based ratios"," net income ratios' and "cash flow ratios";
11. Ratio of (net) operating profit (EBIT) to total gross investment (POA or ROI);
12. Ratio of incremental (net) operating profit to incremental investment (MPOA) or "income variability index" (variability of profitability over time);
13. Ratio of net income or profit after tax (PAT) to share holders" equity/net worth (ROSE).
14. Ratio of (net) income, profit or earnings (EBDIT/EBIT/OCF)to total or tangible) assets (ROA;
15. Ratio of profit before tax (PBT) or profit after tax (PAT) to capital employed (ROCE), or net income to net working/capital, or net income to total debt;
16. Ratio of "present values of inflows" to outlay (PI or B/C ratio);and
17. Ratio of contribution to sales (P/V ratio) as also "interval ratios";

Valuation is the estimation of a firm's worth, "valuation ratios" are also known as "market tests". The market value of equity shares (common stock) is guided mainly by investment instinct and speculative instinct. The following are some of the relevant ratios in this context:

1. Ratio of "market value of equity capital" to "book value of assets" (valuation ratio);
2. Ratio of earnings to equity share capital outstanding, along with the ratio of "cash flow" to tangible assets or net

worth;

3. Ratio of "earnings per share" to "market price of equity share" (E/P ratio);
4. Ratio of "market price of equity share" to earnings per share (P/E ratio);
5. Ratio of dividend per share to paid-up value of share;
6. Ratio of "market price per share" to its "face value"
7. Ratio of "dividend per share" to "market price of share" (yield);
8. Ratio of total dividends to net profit after tax (payout ratio);
9. Ratio of retained profit to net profit after tax (retention ratio);
10. Ratio of retained profit to total assets (total liabilities) or tangible assets (capital employed);
11. Ratio of net liquidation value (adjusted cash position) to equity share capital;
12. Ratio of "retained profit plus depreciation charge" to debt;
13. Ratio of actual earnings to normally expected level of earnings (income capitalization value index or "stability of earnings index";
14. Ratio of super-profit to retained earnings;
15. Ratio of "total market value of stock (equity)" to "total market value of the firm" (or net worth to total assets);
16. Synergy ratios/size ratios; and
17. Retained profit/depreciation ratios.

Questions

1. Examine the relationship between liquidity, solvency and profitability of a firm.
2. The current ratio of a firm is 2.5, whereas its quick ratio is 0.5. Make your own assessment of the firm's liquidity, keeping in view the "rules of thumb".
3. Mark the correct answer in the following set of alternatives:

   Ships are fixed assets for a shipbuilding company

(true/false);

Ships are current assets for a shipping company (true/false);

Chairs and sofa sets used for seating customers are fixed assets for a furniture dealer (true/false);

Buildings constructed for sale are fixed assets for a housing corporation (true/false);

Computers are fixed assets for Indian Airlines and current assets for IBM (true/partly true/false);

Prepaid expenses and inventories are quick assets (true/partly true/false);

Investments in shares and securities are current assets (true/ partly (true/false);

Accounts receivable and inventories are quick assets (true/partly true/false);

Cash in hand and bank deposits are quick assets ('rue/partly true/false); and

Cash in banks, marketable securities, accounts receivable, inventories, and prepaid expenses are current assets (true/partly true/false);

Goodwill, patents, copyrights, preliminary expenses, and accumulated losses are intangible assets (true/partly true/false); and

4. "The ratio of trade creditors to inventories is the most significant relationship." What is the basis of such a statement? Comment thereon and indicate, with reasons, what (in your view) is try most significant measure of liquidity.
5. What do you mean by "activity ratios"? Keeping in view certain well-defined groups of activities, suggest norms of relationships between turnover and inventories.
6. The "debtor's ratio" of a firm has gone up (between two consecutive, accounting years) from 45 to 90 days, whereas the "creditor's ratio" has fallen from 60 to 30 days. How would you interpret these changes, and what norms would you like to establish in this regard?

7. What is meant by "working capital gap"? Examine the alternative approaches in this regard, keeping in view the vital prescriptions.

4

Economic Value Added (EVA) Based Performance Measurement

4.1 Goals of Financial Management

The goal of financial management is to maximize the shareholder's value. The shareholder's wealth is measured by the returns they receive on their investment. Returns are in two parts, first is in the form of dividends and the second in the form of capital appreciation reflected in market value of shares of which market value is thee dominant part. The market value of share is influenced by number of factors, many, of which, may not be fully influenced by the management of firm. However, one factor, which has a significant influence on the market value, is the expectation of the shareholders regarding the return on their investment. There exist very measures like return on capital employed, return on equity, earnings per share, net profit margin, and operating profit margin to evaluate the performance of the business. The problem with theses measures is that they lack a proper benchmark for comparison. The shareholders require at least a minimum rate of return on their vestment depending on the risk in the investment. To overcome these problems the concept of EVA vas developed.

The report studies Indian bank's profile to demonstrate a direct correlation between the investment in stakeholder relationships and corporate performance. Many Indian banking seems to have destroyed shareholder's wealth over a period of time and only a few have positively contributed to their wealth. With the help of EVA (Economic Value Added) which tell what the institution is doing with investor's hard earned money, the report examines an appropriate way of evaluating bank's performance and also finds out which Indian banks have been able to create (or destroy) shareholders wealth since 2005-2006 to 2007-2008.

4.2 What is EVA?

Economic Value Added, EVA for short, is primarily a benchmark to measure earnings efficiency. Though the term "Economic Profit" was very much there since the inception of "Economics", Stern Stewart & Co., of USA has got a registered Trade Mark for this by the name "EVA", an acronym for Economic Value Added. EVA as a residual income measure of financial performance is simply the operating profit after tax less a charge for the capital, equity as well as debt, used in the business. Because EVA includes profit and loss as well as balance sheet efficiency as well as opportunity cost of investor capital- it is better linked to changes in shareholder wealth and is superior to traditional financial metrics such as PAT or percentage rate of return measures such as ROCE or ROE. In addition, EVA is a management tool to focus managers on the impact of their decisions in increasing shareholder wealth. These include both strategic decisions such as what investments to make, which business to exist , what financing structure is optimal; as well as operational decisions involving trade-offs between profit and asset efficiency such as whether to make in house or outsource, repair or replace a piece of equipment , whether to make short or long production runs etc.

Most importantly the real key to increasing shareholder wealth is to integrate the EVA framework in four key areas: to measure business performance; to guide managerial decision making; business literacy throughout the organization. To better align managers interests with shareholders, the EVA framework needs to be holistically applied in an integrated approach–simply measuring EVA is not enough, it must also become the basis of key management decisions as well as be linked to senior management's variable compensation.

4.3 Defining Shareholder's Value and Wealth Creation

From the economist's viewpoint, value is created when management generates revenues over and above the economic costs to generate these revenues. Costs come from four sources: employee wages and benefits; material, supplies, and economic depreciation of physical assets; taxes; and the opportunity cost of using the capital. Under this value-based view, value is only created when revenues exceed all costs including a capital charge. This value accrues mostly to shareholders because they are the residual owners of the firm. Shareholders expect management to generate value over and above the costs of resources consumed, including the cost of using capital. If suppliers of capital do not receive a fair return to compensate them for the risk they are taking, they will withdraw their capital in search of better returns, since value will be lost. A company that is destroying value will always struggle to attract further capital to finance expansion since it will be hamstrung by a share price that stands at a discount to the underlying value of its assets and by higher interest rates on debt or bank loans demanded by creditors.

Wealth creation refers to changes in the wealth of shareholders on a periodic (annual) basis. Applicable to exchange-listed firms, changes in shareholder wealth are inferred mostly from changes in stock prices, dividends paid, and equity raised during the period. Since stock prices reflect investor expectations about future cash flows, creating wealth for shareholders requires that the firm undertake investment decisions that have a positive net present value (NPV).

Although used interchangeably, there is a subtle difference between value creation and wealth creation. The value perspective is based on measuring value directly from accounting-based information with some adjustments, while the wealth perspective relies mainly on stock market information. For a publicly traded firm these two concepts are identical when (i) management provides all pertinent information to capital markets, and (ii) the markets believe and have confidence in management.

4.4 Calculation of EVA

The company creates shareholders value only if it generates returns in excess of its cost of capital. The excess of returns over cost of capital is simply termed as Economic Value Added. To put in a simple terms EVA is the profits generated by any economic entity over its cost of capital employed. The entity can be a company, country or the entire human civilization. If the difference between the above two parameters is positive than the entity is said to be creating wealth for its stakeholders. A negative EVA on the other hand indicates the company is a destroyer of value.

EVA is just a way of measuring an operation's real profitability. EVA holds a company accountable for the cost of capital it uses to expand and operate its business and attempts to show whether a company is creating a real value for its shareholders

Just earning profit is not enough, a business should earn sufficient profit to cover its cost of capital and create surplus to grow. Stated simply, any profit earned over and above the cost of capital is Economic Value Added. Traditionally the methods of measurement of corporate performance are many. Common bases used are: Net Profit Margin (NPM), Operating Profit Margin (OPM), Return on Investment (ROI) and Return on Net Worth (RONW). Profit After Tax (PAT) is an indicator of profit available to the shareholder and Profit Before Interest After Tax (PBIAT) is an indicator of the surplus generated using total funds. ROI is still recognized as the most popular yardstick of profitability measurement. However, the traditionally used profit indicators are ineffective parameters in explaining whether the reported profit covers the cost of capital. Old profit concept fails to indicate clear surplus. The basic proposition is that the Return on Capital Employed should be greater than the Cost of Capital (i.e. ROCE > K0). Capital employed highlights long-term capital and cost of capital represents weighted average cost of capital.

Traditionally, Profit after Tax is shown in the Profit and Loss Account to indicate the profit available to the shareholders, both preference and equity. Ability to maintain dividend is not a test of profit adequacy. Ability to generate Economic Value Added is the only test of profit adequacy. Any surplus generated from operating activities over and above the cost of capital is termed as EVA. It is a new measure of corporate surplus that should be shared by the employees, management and shareholders. EVA focuses on clear surplus in contradiction to the traditionally used profit available to the shareholders. It is used by companies as a performance indicator and also as a basis for executive compensation. Surplus should be derived by deducting cost of capital from profit before interest but after tax.

EVA = NOPAT – WACC × Capital Employed.

Where, NOPAT means Net Operating Profit before Interest and after Tax.

WACC represents Weighted Average Cost of Capital.

Capital Employed = Net Block + Trading Investment + Net Current Assets.

It is free from subjective assumption that needs to be adopted while identifying profit and cost of capital. Cost of equity is derived on the basis of Capital Assets Pricing Model (CAPM). The founders of EVA traditionally use CAPM. Under CAPM Cost of Equity (Ke) is given by the following

Ke = Rf + (Rm – Rf)

Where, Rf = Risk free return.

Rm = Market expected Rate of Return

= Risk Co-efficient.

Both market return and Beta are highly volatile, and if annual market return and yearly beta of a company are chosen for finding cost of equity, abnormally high or low market related cost of equity may be obtained. To avoid this difficulty, one may apply "Long run approach". While deriving EVA it becomes necessary to make certain accounting adjustments, which are required only for corporate reporting purposes. It is sometimes alleged that EVA talks too much about the shareholders value added rather than focusing on the interest of all stakeholders. But EVA is a powerful performance measurement tool and it is argued that if a company is able to serve its shareholders then it can better serve all other stakeholders also.

4.5 Benefits of EVA for Banks

As banks become 'capital hungry' to meet their growth expectations and simultaneously meeting the regulatory requirements in the Basel-II era, they would have to remain responsive to the expectations of the market on a risk adjusted basis to ensure continued supply of financial capital from the shareholders and human capital from the ultimate stakeholders. One of the fundamental limitations in the existing business growth strategies of Indian banks, especially public sector banks, is its virtual, if not complete, disconnect with riskiness. 'Profit rich but Risk poor' strategies are doomed for failure in the long-run! Finalization of business targets should no longer remain a mundane 'volume-mix' targeting exercise but should built-in inherent risk-return dimensions.

Business strategies that ensure 'Risk and Return by Choice and not by Chance' are key to ensure continuing success of banks in the emerging market. In order to align the performance of individual zones/regions/branches to the overall corporate expectations in terms of EVA, the vocabulary of risk management has to percolate down the hierarchy of banks to the individual unit level. New performance benchmarks in the form of EVA should naturally form the unifying cord/link in every bank. EVA can be an important tool that bankers can use to measure and improve the financial performance of their bank. Since EVA takes the interest of the bank's shareholders into consideration, the use of EVA by bank management may lead to different decisions than if management relied solely on other measures. As mentioned earlier an important difference between banks and others is the role of debt.

For other firms debt is a part of the financing operations and interest expenses are excluded from Net Operating Profit after Taxes (NOPAT) so that returns are unlevered. A bank's debt funding is effectively the raw material which is intermediated into higher yielding assets. Interest expense, on this view, is equivalent of the cost of goods sold. This has an important consequence. In our analysis, NOPAT for each year was therefore arrived at after adding interest on RBI loans and other loans to Profit before Depreciation and Taxes less Cash Taxes. The component of cash taxes represented as if banks were debt free. In order to calculate cash taxes, tax shield on the interest paid on RBI loans and others were added back to Tax Provision and tax paid on other incomes were deducted from tax provision of the year. A tax rate of 30 percent per year was assumed for maintaining consistency over years in our analysis. The economic capital of a bank is defined as the shareholders funds plus reserves excluded from equity, such as loan losses or contingency reserve which in economic terms, function as capital. In this fund total long term borrowings of the bank are added to arrive at the Invested Capital (IC). In our analysis we have first attempted to critically evaluate bank's performance in generating Return on Invested Capital (ROIC) over years, we have taken two most critical indicators viz. Return on Invested Capital (ROIC) and Incremental ROIC.

4.6 Limitations of Traditional Methods

Most of the accounting based measures such as Price Earnings, Book Value, Returns on Equity, Return on Net worth etc. fail to provide a clear understanding of the major variables that drive value, except to some extent Returns on Invested Capital. These methods are easily influenced by the smart and perhaps mischievous management through window dressings. They also do not incorporate risk or time value of money also and do not help investors understand the intricate process of value creation. In addition, these traditional measures use, for most part, historical data to measure current performance. Ideally, one would like to measure how current decisions will affect the firm's future performance. Unlike accounting measures, Economic Value Added, raises the issue highlighted in the Nobel Prize work of Franco Modigliani and Merton Miller: just as debt holders of a bank expect a specific return, the shareholders of the bank, expect a certain rate of return for taking risk of investing in the bank.

4.7 EVA a Superior Performance Measure

First let us look into the claim of EVA being superior than the conventional measures such as ROI, ROE and ROA, which are based on the accounting figures. Most of these measures give us the rate of return earned by the bank with respect to capital invested in the bank. The most important limitation of these measures is derived from limitations inherent in the measurement of accounting profit. As per current accounting practices, while historical-cost-based accounting measures are being used to carry most of the assets in the balance sheet, revenue and expenses (other than depreciation) are recognized in the profit and loss account at their current value. Therefore accounting rate of returns do not reflect the true return from an investment and tend to be biased downwards in the 10 initial years and upwards in the latter years. Similarly as noted by Malkelainen (Esa Malkelainen 1998), distortion occurs basically due to the historical cost and straight line depreciation schedule used by most businesses to value their assets.

This leads to a bias in these measures due to the composition of assets of a bank at any given point in time. By composition he refers to the current nature of the assets, more current the assets are, the accounting rate of return is closer to the true rate of return. This distortion will not be significant if there is a continuous stream of investments in assets i.e. the value of the mix of assets is nearer to the current value of the assets. But the probability, that at any point of time, a bank should have such a composition of assets is rare, in most cases either the assets are old or relatively new. This precludes these accounting measures from being used to reach any meaningful conclusion regarding the true performance of the bank. The other important limitation of accounting measures is that they ignore the cost of equity and only consider the borrowing cost. As a result it ignores the risk inherent in the project and fails to highlight whether the return is commensurate with the risk of the underlying assets.

This might result in selecting projects that produce attractive rate of return but destroys bank value because their cost of capital is higher than the benchmark return established by the management. On the other hand accounting measures encourage managers to select projects that will improve the current rate of return and to ignore projects even if their return is higher than their cost of capital. Selection of projects with returns higher than the current rate of return does not automatically increase shareholders' wealth. Taking up only those projects, which provide returns that are higher than the hurdle rate (cost of capital) results in increasing the wealth of the shareholder. Therefore, use of ROE, ROA or similar accounting measures as the benchmark, might result in selection of those projects that though provide rate of return higher than the current rate of return destroys bank-value. Similarly use of these measures result in continuing with activities that destroys bank value until the rate of return falls below the benchmark rate of return.

EVA proponents claim that because of these imperfections, the accounting based measures are not good proxies for value creation. Managerial compensation based on these measures does not encourage value enhancement actions by managers. Value enhancement and earnings are two different things and might be at cross-purposes because short-term performance might be improved at the cost of long term health of the bank. Activities involving enhancement of current earnings may be short term in nature, whereas any value enhancing activities should focus on long term well being of the bank.

Avoidance of discretionary costs improves current performance while destroying value of the bank. The question arises whether EVA is an improvement over conventional measures and serves the purpose of motivating managers to pay attention to shareholders value even if that results in compromising current performance. The answer may be negative because all the above limitations are also associated with EVA. As shown in equation, the calculation of EVA entails the usage of an accounting rate of return, the difference lies only in the fact that the cost of equity is also factored in to arrive at the residual income figure. Though incorporation of the cost of equity capital is the virtue of EVA, because it measures economic surplus, it does not remove the limitations of the accounting profit that forms the basis for computing EVA.

Moreover the virtue might not be realized in practice since it is not easy to calculate the cost of equity. Market returns cannot be used as a proxy for cost of equity that supports assets in place because market discounts the expectations. Similarly it is difficult to use CAPM in measuring cost of equity because it is difficult to measure risk-free-rate of return, beta and market premium. Difficulties get compounded in an economic environment like India, where interest rates fluctuate frequently, the capital market is volatile and the regulators are yet to have a complete grip on the capital market to enhance its efficiency. Empirical studies show that the volatility in the Indian capital markets, like capital markets in other developing economies, is higher than capital markets in developed economies. Therefore even if for the sake of argument it can be said that the potential of EVA as a measure of performance can be realized fully in an advanced economy, the argument that EVA is a better measure is not tenable in the Indian context.

References

Al Ebrhar and G. Bennett Stewart III (1999). The EVA revolution; Journal of Applied Corporate Finance Vol 12, No.2.

Al Ebrhar, Gary Hamel (1997). Debate: Duking it out over EVA; Fortune, Chicago, p. 232.

Alfred Rappaport (1986).Creating Shareholder Value, The New Standard for Business Performance; The Free Press.

Aswati Damodaran (1998). Value Creation and Enhancement: Back to the future; Working paper series; Stern School of Business.

Bacidore, Jeffrey M, Boquist, John A, Milbourn, Todd T, Thakor, Anjan V.(1997). The search for the best financial performance measure; Financial Analysts Journal Charlottesville, pp. 11-20.

Banerjee, Ashok (1999). Economic Value Added and shareholder wealth: An Empirical examination; Paradigm, Vol. 3 No.1, pp. 99-133.

Bennett III, Stewart G (1995). EVA works: but not if you make these common mistakes; Fortune, Chicago, pp. 117-118.

Biddle, Bowen & Wallace, Evidence on EVA (1999). Journal of Applied Corporate Finance, Volume 12, No. 2.

Websites

http://www.banknetindia.com/banking/boverview.htm.

http://rbidocs.rbi.org.in/rdocs/Publications/DOCs/87122.xls.

http://www.hdfcbank.com/

http://www.rbi.org.in.

http://www.statebankofindia.com/

5

Performance Evaluation of Select Banks by Camel Model

5.1 Introduction

Many firms in the service industry face the problem of disparate results in terms of efficiency. This problem is a cause of concern for many big organizations such as banks, hotels, courier companies, and so on. In particular, the last decade has witnessed continuous changes in regulation, technology and competition in the global financial services industry, and Indian banks are no exception. Rising cost-income ratios and declining profitability reflect increased competitive pressure. To assess the stability of the banking system, it is therefore crucial to benchmark the performance of banks operating in India. An efficient banking system contributes in an extensive way to higher economic growth in any country. Thus, studies of banking efficiency are very important for policy makers, industry leaders and many others who are reliant on the banking sector.

The present study is important because enhancing performance of banks has been the key objective of financial sector reforms in many countries and India is not the exception to the above. For this purpose, the CAMEL model was used. The issues that have been addressed in this study are: How the banks (i.e. public and private sector) have fared in the four years of twenty first century? Is there any significant variation between the performances of these banks? Whether the performance of these four banks in terms of various parameters such as Capital Adequacy, Assets Quality, Management, Efficiency and Liquidity have improved in the recent past?

A sound financial system is essential for a healthy and

vibrant economy. The banking sector constitutes a predominant component of the financial services industry and the performance of any economy, to a large extent, is dependent on the performance of banks. Banking institutions in our country have been assigned a significant role in financing the process of planned economic growth. In 1969, fourteen banks were nationalized with the objectives of extending the credit facilities to all segments of the economy and also to mitigate seasonal imbalances in its availability. Since nationalization the banking system of India has witnessed structural and dimensional changes. A number of steps were taken in close succession, enabling the nationalized banks to play an active role in economic development. The second step in the process of nationalizing the banks was taken in 1980, when six other major banks were nationalized. Directed interest rates on deposits and lending, exchange controls, directed credit became hallmark of this tightly regulated new structure.

Following the balance of payments crisis in 1991-92, wide ranging reforms were initiated in almost all the spheres of the economy including real sector, external sector, agricultural and industrial sector, macro-economic policy, public sector disinvestment etc. The objectives of the financial sector reforms were to bring about greater efficiency and competitiveness in all the spheres of the economic activity.

A decade and a half have gone since the initiation of banking sector reforms in India. Over this period, the Indian banking sector has experienced a paradigm shift. Hence, it is high time to make performance appraisal of this sector. It is against the above background that the present study has been conducted.

A study such as this is important because enhancing performance of banks has been the key objective of financial sector reforms in many countries. And India is not the exception to the above.

5.2 Objectives

1. To know the financial efficiency of selected banks.
2. To analyzed any significant variation between the performances of these banks.
3. To examine the performance of these four banks in terms of various parameters such as Capital Adequacy, Assets Quality, Management Efficiency and Liquidity have improved in the recent past.
4. To summarize the main findings of the study by offering suitable suggestions.
5. To find out the financially strong and weak points of selected banks.

5.3 Hypothesis for the Research

The Null Hypothesis (H_0): *"The performance of Private Banks is better than Nationalized Banks"*

The Alternate Hypothesis (H_1): *"The performance of Nationalized Banks is better than Private Banks"*

5.4 Scope of the Study and Data Collection

The scope of this research is limited to selected four banks. This research will be helpful to banks while doing competitors analysis.

This will help the banks to frame effective Financial Strategy.

The period for evaluating performance through CAMEL in this study, ranges from 2002-03 to 2005-06 i.e. for 4 years. The data is collected from various sources such as Annual Reports of the Banks, Indian Banking Association Journal, Reserve Bank of India (RBI) Bulletin, Journal of Banking Studies, Journal of Accounting and Finance and Indian Journal of Commerce. Internet has been an important source of secondary data. The site assessed for this research was www.rbi.org.in.

5.5 Review of Literature

Basel II accord is already in vogue for implementation by

March 2007. The accord stands on three pillars: (a) Risk Management, (b) Supervisory Function, and (c) Discipline. The supervisory strategy in India at present comprises both off-site surveillance and on-site inspections and control system internal to banks. A detailed off-site surveillance system based on 'prudential' supervisory reporting framework on a quarterly basis covering capital adequacy, asset quality, loan concentration, operational results and connected lending has been made operational. This is combined with a verification of prudent practices and financial condition of banks through on-site examination. The approach to on-site inspection of banks in accordance with the recommendations of the Padmanabhan Working Group (1995) has been adopted from the cycle of inspections commencing July 1997. It focuses on the mandated aspects of solvency, liquidity, financial and operational health, based on a modified version of the CAMEL model viz., CAMELS, which evaluates banks' Capital Adequacy, Asset Quality, Management, Earnings, Liquidity and Systems and Control, shedding the audit elements under the existing inspection system.

Padmanabhan Working Group (1995), on On-Site Supervision in its report recommended for supervisory interventions and introduction of a rating methodology for banks on the lines of CAMEL model with appropriate modification to suit Indian conditions. The Working Group has recommended six rating factors namely-Capital Adequacy, Assets Quality, Management, Earnings, Liquidity, Systems and Controls (i.e. CAMELS) and for Foreign Banks four rating factors, namely–Capital Adequacy, Assets Quality, Compliance, Systems and Controls (i.e. CACS). *Narasimham Committee (1998)* made several important recommendations like introduction of internationally accepted prudential norms relating to income recognition, assets classification, provisioning and capital adequacy. Accordingly, a framework for the evaluation of the current strength of the system and of the operations and performance of banks has been provided by

Reserve Bank's measuring rod of "CAMELS" which stands for Capital Adequacy, Assets Quality, Management, Earnings, Liquidity and internal Control Systems.

Thus the present supervisory system in banking sector is a substantial improvement over the earlier system in terms of frequency, coverage and focus as also the tools employed. Nearly one-half of the Basel Core Principles for Effective Banking Supervision has already been adhered to and the remaining is at different stages of implementation. Two Supervisory Rating Models based on CAMELS and CACS (capital adequacy, asset quality, compliance and systems) factors for rating of Indian commercial banks and foreign banks operating in India respectively, have been worked out on the lines recommended by the Padmanabhan Working Group (1995). These ratings would enable the Reserve Bank to identify the banks whose condition warrants special supervisory attention.

To build the conceptual framework for the application of CAMEL Model we may draw on the following literature.

Barr and Siems (1996) tried to predict bank failures in US, using the data from December 1984 to June 1987 using CAMEL Model. They used technical efficiency measure using DEA in their prediction model. Along with their DEA results which represent Management Quality "M" in the CAMEL rating, they used financial ratios representing soundness of Capital, Asset Quality, Earnings and Liquidity. They found that using the DEA Efficiency Score in the regression increased the accuracy of the classification results from 89 percent to 92.4 percent and the new model was superior to the earlier early-warning models.

Godse (1996) examined the application of new model CAMEL i.e. "Capital Adequacy, Assets Quality, Management, Earning Quality, Liquidity, Systems and Control" for evaluating the performance of banks.

Rao and Datta (1998) made an attempt to derive rating based on CAMEL. In their study, based on these five groups

(C-A-M-E-L), in all 21 parameters were developed. After deriving separate rating for each parameter a combined rating was derived for all nationalized banks (19) for the year 1998. The study found that Corporation Bank has the best rating followed by Oriental Bank of Commerce, Bank of Baroda, Dena Bank and Punjab National Bank etc. And the worst rating was found to be of Indian Bank preceded by UCO Bank, United Bank of India, Syndicate Bank and Vijaya Bank.

Camel Model

C- Capital Adequacy	Capital Adequacy Ratio Debt-Equity Ratio Advances to Assets G-Secs to Total Investments
A- Assets Quality	Gross NPAs to Net Advances Net NPAs to Net Advances Total Investments to Total Assets Percentage change in Net NPAs Net NPAs to Total Assets
M- Management	Profit per Branch Total Advances to Total Deposits Business per Employee Profit per Employee
E- Earning Quality	Operating Profits to Average Working Funds Percentage Growth in Net Profits Spread Net Profit to Average Assets Interest Income to Total Income Non-Interest Income to Total Income
L- Liquidity	Liquid Assets to Total Assets G-Secs to Total Assets Liquid Assets to Demand Deposits Liquid Assets to Total Deposits

Prasuna (2004) analyzed the performance of Indian banks

by adopting CAMEL Model. The performance of 65 banks was studied for the period 2003-04. The author concluded that the competition is tough and consumers are benefited from it. Better services quality, innovative products, better bargains are all greeting the Indian customers. The coming fiscal will prove to be a transition phase for Indian banks, as they will have to align their strategic focus to increasing interest rates.

Veni (2004) studied the capital adequacy requirement of banks and the measures adopted by them to strengthen their capital ratios. The author highlighted that the rating agencies give prominence to Capital Adequacy Ratios of banks while rating the bank's certificate of deposits, fixed deposits and bonds. They normally adopt CAMEL Model for rating banks. Thus Capital Adequacy is considered as key element of bank rating.

Satish, Jutur and Surender (2005) adopted CAMEL model to assess the performance of Indian banks. The author analyzed the performance of 55 banks for the year 2004-05 by using CAMEL Model. They concluded that the Indian Banking system looks sound and Information Technology will help the banking system grow in strength going into future. Banks Initial Public Offer will be hitting the market to increase their capital and gearing up for the Basel II norms.

5.6 Capital Adequacy Analysis

It is important for a bank to maintain depositors' confidence and prevent the bank from going bankrupt. *Capital* is seen as a cushion to protect depositors and promote the stability and efficiency of financial system around the world. *Capital Adequacy* reflects the overall financial condition of the banks and also the ability of the management to meet the need for additional capital. It also indicates whether the bank has enough capital to absorb unexpected losses. Capital Adequacy Ratios act as indicators of bank leverage. The following ratios measure capital adequacy.

5.6.1 Capital Adequacy Ratio (CAR): The banks are

required to maintain the Capital Adequacy Ratio (CAR) as specified by RBI from time to time. As per the latest RBI norms, the banks in India should have a CAR of 9 percent. It is arrived at by dividing the sum of Tier-I, Tier-II and Tier-III capital by aggregate of Risk Weighted Assets (RWA) (Table 5.1). Symbolically:

CAR= (Tier-I + Tier-II + Tier-III)/RWA

Tier-I capital includes equity capital and free reserves.

Tier-II capital comprises of subordinate debt of 5-7 years tenure, revaluation reserves, general provisions and loss reserves, hybrid debt capital instruments and undisclosed reserves and cumulative perpetual preference shares.

Tier-III capital comprises of short-term subordinate debt.

The higher the CAR, the stronger is considered a bank as it ensures high safety against bankruptcy.

Table 5.1: Capital to Risk Weighted Assets Ratio of Selected Banks

Bank	2002-03	2003-04	2004-05	2005-06	Average
ICICI Bank	13.5	13.53	12.45	11.88	12.84
SBI Bank	11.1	10.36	11.78	13.35	11.65
IndusInd Bank	12.13	12.75	11.62	10.54	11.76
Dena Bank	6.02	9.48	11.91	10.62	9.51

As per the latest RBI norms, the banks in India should have a CAR of 9 percent. All banks were capable enough to maintain 9 percent during last 4 years except in 2002-03 while Dena Bank could not maintain that but it shows healthy improvement in 2003-04 than the previous year. Here, all banks have shown fluctuation in maintaining but all have the good margins than required. The higher the CAR, the stronger is considered a bank as it ensures high safety against bankruptcy. So we can say that ICICI is highest CAR from 2002-03 to 2004-05 but in last year SBI takes its position by maintaining CAR at 13.35 percent.

5.6.2 Debt-Equity Ratio: This ratio indicates the degree of leverage of a bank. It indicates how much of the bank business is financed through debt and how much through equity. This is calculated as the proportion of total outside liability to net worth. *Outside Liabilities* includes total borrowings, deposits and other liabilities. *Net Worth* includes equity capital and reserves and surplus. Higher ratio indicates less protection for the creditors and depositors in the banking system (Table 5.2).

Table 5.2: Debt-Equity Ratio (times) of Selected Banks

Bank	2002-03	2003-04	2004-05	2005-06	Average
ICICI Bank	11.32	11.82	10.34	12.19	11.42
SBI	17.75	16.41	16.04	15.03	16.31
IndusInd Bank	6.48	17.85	17.84	19.5	15.38
Dena Bank	19.19	20.00	20.77	18.82	19.70

Higher ratio indicates less protection for the creditors and depositors in the banking system. Here, all the four banks are maintaining below 50, indicating that all banks are not over leveraged. Dena Bank has maintaining higher than the other banks, meaning it is not secure than other banks.

5.6.3 Advances to Assets Ratio: This is the ratio of the Total Advances to Total Assets. This ratio indicates a bank's aggressiveness in lending which ultimately results in better profitability. Higher ratio of advances/deposits (assets) is preferred to a lower one. Total advances also include receivables. The value of total assets is excluding the revaluation of all the assets (Table 5.3).

In the year 2004-05, IndusInd Bank had the highest by providing 57.61 percent advances against the assets, while in the next year ICICI took its place by 55.03 percent. Here, we can interpret that private banks are aggressive in lending than nationalized banks which ultimately give them higher profitability.

Table 5.3: Advances to Assets Ratio (Percent) of Selected Banks

Bank	2002-03	2003-04	2004-05	2005-06	Average
ICICI Bank	49.88	49.59	54.52	55.03	52.26
SBI	36.65	38.73	44.01	45.63	41.26
IndusInd Bank	54.01	48.40	57.61	52.83	53.21
Dena Bank	41.83	42.47	47.06	53.61	46.24

5.6.4 Government Securities to Total Investments: The percentage of investment in government securities to total investments is a very important indicator which shows the risk-taking ability of a bank. It indicates a bank's strategy as being high profit-high risk or low profits-low risk. It also gives a view as to the availability of alternative investment opportunities. Government securities are generally considered as the most safe debt instrument, which as a result carries the lowest return. Since government securities are risk free, the higher the Government securities to investment ratio, the lower the risk involved in a bank's investments (Table 5.4).

Table 5.4: Government Securities to Total Investment Ratio (Percent) of Selected Banks

Bank	2002-03	2003-04	2004-05	2005-06	Average
ICICI Bank	72.05	69.96	68.31	69.53	69.96
SBI	83.61	84.85	87.24	88.19	85.97
IndusInd Bank	79.68	84.10	83.68	84.72	83.05
Dena Bank	70.34	78.07	81.97	82.03	78.10

This ratio indicates many things like strategy of the banks, risk-taking capacity and profitability.

ICICI Bank and Dena Bank followed the high profit- high risk strategy, while SBI and IndusInd Bank, ICICI Bank and Dena Bank followed the low profit-low risk strategy. SBI gives the highest safety than the other banks but with low return. We can say that SBI and IndusInd Bank are more conservative than the ICICI Bank and Dena Bank. In the year 2004-05, SBI Bank had the highest safety by investing 88.19 percent in government securities; the highest fluctuation witnessed was in 2003-04 was in the case of Dena bank from 70.34 percent to 78.07 percent and IndusInd Bank from 79.6 percent to 84.10 percent.

The quality of assets is an important parameter to gauge the strength of a bank. The prime motto behind measuring the assets quality is to ascertain the component of non-performing assets (NPA) as a percentage of the total assets. This indicates what types of advances the bank has made to generate interest income. Thus, assets quality indicates the type of debtors, the bank is having. The following ratios are necessary to assess assets quality.

5.6.5 Gross NPAs to Net Advances: It is a measure of the quality of assets in a situation, where the management has not provided for loss on NPAs. Here, the Gross NPAs are measured as a percentage of Net Advances. The lower the ratio, the better the quality of advances (Table 5.5).

Table 5.5: Gross NPAs to Net Advances Ratio (Percent) of Selected Banks

Bank	2002-03	2003-04	2004-05	2005-06	Average
ICICI Bank	9.44	4.91	3.03	4.83	5.55
SBI	9.80	8.02	6.15	7.05	7.76
IndusInd Bank	4.98	3.55	3.56	2.89	3.75
Dena Bank	19.16	15.77	6.67	10.15	12.94

Data describes that IndusInd Bank and ICICI Bank gave better quality of advances than other banks which interprets that quality of assets is better with private banks than with the nationalized banks.

5.6.6 Net NPAs to Net Advances: It is most standard

measure of assets quality. In this ratio, Net NPAs are measured as a percentage of Net Advances. Net NPAs are Gross NPAs net of provisions on NPAs and interest in suspense account Table 5.6).

Table 5.6: Net NPAs to Net Advances Ratio of Selected Banks

Bank	2002-03	2003-04	2004-05	2005-06	Average
ICICI Bank	5.21	2.21	1.65	0.72	2.45
SBI	4.5	3.48	2.65	1.48	3.03
IndusInd Bank	3.18	2.9	1.78	1.37	2.31
Dena Bank	2.31	2.97	1.35	1.83	2.12

The above data describes that ICICI Bank had better results of net NPA's to net advances than other banks which interprets that net profitability and productivity is far better than in any other bank. This ratio is more accountable especially for any bank in this competitive era especially in the co-operative banks.

5.6.7 Total Investments to Total Assets Ratio: Total investment to total assets indicates the extent of deployment of assets in investment as against advances. This ratio is used as a tool to measure the percentage of total assets locked up in investments, which by conventional definition, does not form part of the core income of a bank. A higher level of investment means lack of credit off-take in the economy. This ratio is calculated by dividing total investments by total assets of a bank. A higher ratio means that the bank has conservatively kept a high cushion of investments to guard against NPAs. However, this affects its profitability adversely (Table 5.7).

SBI and Dena Bank invest more to manage NPAs but it causes the lack of credit off-take and ultimately it affects the profitability of the bank. SBI's investment was the highest than other banks in last 4 years but it gave more safety. The result shows high ratio for SBI being a government sector bank, while the same is very low for private sector banks.

Table 5.7: Total Investments to Total Assets Ratio (Percent) of Selected Banks

Bank	2002-03	2003-04	2004-05	2005-06	Average
ICICI Bank	33.20	34.13	30.11	32.15	32.40
SBI	45.85	45.53	42.86	43.65	44.47
IndusInd Bank	25.60	30.19	26.05	30.70	28.14
Dena Bank	42.16	43.94	40.36	32.29	39.69

5.6.8 Percentage Change in Net NPAs: It is a very important indicator of the way the bank is working on the recovery of its NPAs or writing off these NPAs and improving the balance sheet. This measure presents the movement in net NPAs on year-to-year basis. The lower the percentage change, the better the quality of assets (Table 5.8).

Table 5.8: Percentage change in Net NPAs Ratio (Percent) of Selected Banks

Bank	2002-03	2003-04	2004-05	2005-06	Average
ICICI Bank		-49.61	5.76	30.06	-4.60
SBI	9.21	11.98	1.71	8.27	7.79
IndusInd Bank	38.08	6.59	-15.04	20.18	12.45
Dena Bank	10.59	11.32	33.17	26.76	20.46

From the table we can say that SBI has improved its balance sheet by year-to-year basis and quality of the assets of SBI is better than other banks because the changes in net NPA is very low. While IndusInd Bank and ICICI Bank cannot manage their NPA properly, it fluctuates very highly.

5.6.9 Net NPAs to Total Assets: This ratio indicates the efficiency of the bank in assessing credit risk and to an extent recovering the debts. This ratio is arrived by dividing the net NPAs by total assets. Total assets are considered are net of revaluation reserves. Lower the ratio, better is the performance of the bank (Table 5.9).

From the data we can interpret that SBI is capable enough to assess credit risk and to an extent recover the debts, while Dena Bank is not so capable. From the year 2002-03, ICICI Bank and IndusInd Bank have improved their performance as can be judged by the ratio, which is decreasing every year. Here we can tell that all banks are capable enough to manage credit risk and to recover but than also in year 2002-03, Dena Bank's performance was somewhat poor.

Table 5.9: Net NPAs to Total Assets Ratio (Percent) of Selected Banks

Bank	2002-03	2003-04	2004-05	2005-06	Average
ICICI Bank	2.64	1.14	0.90	1.23	1.48
SBI	1.64	1.33	1.16	1.19	1.33
IndusInd Bank	2.80	1.41	1.56	1.11	1.72
Dena Bank	4.95	3.99	2.46	1.63	3.26

Management efficiency is another important element of the CAMEL Model. The ratios in this segment involve subjective analysis to measure the efficiency and effectiveness of management. The management of the bank takes crucial decisions depending on its risk perception. It sets vision and goals for the organization and sees that it achieves them. This parameter is used to evaluate management efficiency as to assign premium to better quality banks and discount poorly managed ones. The ratios used to evaluate management efficiency are described as under.

5.6.10 Profit per Branch: This ratio measures the efficiency of the employees at the branch level. It also gives valuable inputs to assess the real strength of a bank's branch network; the higher the ratio, the higher the efficiency of the management.

However, it is advisable to look at the number of branches too, as a bank with fewer branches can figure among the top players in this category despite earning a lower net profit

(Table 5.10).

SBI's performance is best from last year than other banks; it gives an average Rs. 373.26 lakh while comparatively, ICICI Bank's performance is very poor. So, we can predicate that nationalized bank's performance is better than the private bank.

Table 5.10: Profit per Branch Ratio (Lakh) of Selected Branch

Bank	2002-03	2003-04	2004-05	2005-06	Average
ICICI Bank	34.23	40.42	46.99	47.54	42.30
SBI	330.41	390.69	386.32	385.62	373.26
IndusInd Bank	49.26	53.19	54.36	57.12	53.28
Dena Bank	146.94	152.64	155.36	159.19	153.53

5.6.11 Total Advances to Total Deposits: This ratio measures the efficiency and ability of the bank's management in converting the deposits available with the bank (excluding other funds like equity capital etc.) into high earning advances. Total deposits include demand deposits, saving deposits, term deposits and deposits of other banks. Total advances also includes the receivables (Table 5.11).

Table 5.11: Total Advances to Total Deposits Ratio (Percent) of Selected Banks

Bank	2002-03	2003-04	2004-05	2005-06	Average
ICICI Bank	46.52	49.57	55.24	54.23	51.37
SBI	110.61	91.17	91.57	92.15	96.38
IndusInd Bank	62.20	65.19	68.53	62.04	64.52
Dena Bank	51.15	51.29	54.12	60.24	54.20

From the above data we can tell that SBI has better capacity to convert deposits into advances, giving higher profit than the other banks. Data shows that ICICI Bank and Dena Bank are trying to perform well on year-to-year basis. In 2005-

06, the performance of IndusInd Bank was lower than the previous year; it decreased from 68.53 percent to 62.01 percent.

5.6.12 Business per Employee: This ratio shows the productivity of human forces of the bank. It is used as a tool to measure the efficiency of all the employees of a bank in generating business for the bank. It is arrived at by dividing the total business by total number of employees. Higher the ratio, better it is for the bank. By business we mean the sum of total deposits and total advances in a particular year (Table 5.12).

Table 5.12: Business per Employee Ratio (Lakh) of Selected Banks

Bank	2002-03	2003-04	2004-05	2005-06	Average
ICICI Bank	11.2	10.10	8.80	9.05	9.79
SBI	1.91	2.10	2.43	2.99	2.36
IndusInd Bank	12.84	10.80	9.26	8.80	10.43
Dena Bank	2.42	2.74	3.13	3.64	2.98

This ratio shows the ability of employee to take business in the bank, data shows that both IndusInd bank and ICICI Bank's employee gives better business than the Dena Bank and SBI. In the year 2002-03, IndusInd Bank gave the highest business than other banks. The performance of private banks is therefore better than public sector banks just because of the efficiency and ability of employees. While SBI and Dena Bank are trying to perform good their business on year to year basis has increased while ICICI and IndusInd performance year by year has decreased.

5.6.13 Profit per Employee: This ratio shows the surplus earned per employee. It is arrived at by dividing the profit after tax (PAT) earned by the bank by total number of employees. Higher the ratio, higher the efficiency of management (Table 5.13).

Table 5.13: Profit per Employee Ratio (Lakh) of Selected Banks

Bank	2002-03	2003-04	2004-05	2005-06	Average
ICICI Bank	0.11	0.12	0.11	0.10	0.11
SBI	0.01	0.02	0.02	0.02	0.02
IndusInd Bank	0.10	0.15	0.10	0.02	0.09
Dena Bank	0.01	0.02	0.01	0.01	0.02

In the year 2005-06, IndusInd Bank's profitability decreased from Rs. 10,000 to Rs. 2,000, meaning its performance in 2005-06 was very poor. From 2003-04 to 2005-06, ICICI Bank, IndusInd Bank and Dena Bank's performance decreased year to year basis but only SBI maintained its profitability.

The quality of earnings is a very important criterion since that will determine the ability of a bank to earn consistently, going into the future. It basically determines the profitability of the banks. It also explains the sustainability and growth in earnings in the future. This parameter gains importance in the light of the argument that much of a bank's income is earned through non-core activities like investments, treasury operations, corporate advisory services and so on. The following ratios try to assess the quality of income in terms of income generated by core activity-income from lending operations.

5.6.14 Operating Profits to Average Working Funds Ratio: This ratio indicates how much a bank can earn from its operations net of the operating expenses for every rupee spent on working funds. This is arrived at by dividing the operating profits by average working funds. Average Working Funds (AWF) are the total resources (total assets or liabilities) employed by a bank. It is daily average of total assets/ liabilities during a year. The higher the ratio, the better it is. This ratio determines the operating profits generated out of working funds employed. Better utilization of fund will result in higher operating profits. Thus, this ratio will indicate how a bank has employed its working funds in generating profits. Banks which use their assets efficiently will tend to have a better average than the industry average (Table 5.14).

Table 5.14: Operating Profits to Average Working Funds Ratio (Percent) of Selected Banks

Bank	2002-03	2003-04	2004-05	2005-06	Average
ICICI Bank	2.49	2.09	2.18	2.39	2.29
SBI	2.27	2.50	2.61	2.27	2.41
IndusInd Bank	4	3.74	2.87	1.38	2.99
Dena Bank	2.61	3.41	1.94	2.48	2.61

ICICI Bank and SBI maintained their profits from operations during last 4 years but IndusInd Bank and Dena Bank fluctuated. We can say that performance of IndusInd Bank has decreased while that of ICICI has increased. But we can interpret that all banks get good profit from their operation work.

5.6.15 Percentage Growth in Net Profits: Percentage change in net profit over the previous year is another parameter of earning quality measurement (Table 5.15).

Table 5.15: Percentage Growth in Net Profits of Selected Banks

Bank	2002-03	2003-04	2004-05	2005-06	Average
ICICI Bank	367.44	35.74	22.48	26.67	113.08
SBI	27.67	18.55	16.95	2.37	16.39
IndusInd Bank	77.67	190.63	-19.81	-82.48	41.50
Dena Bank	905.19	101.86	-73.54	19.66	238.29

From data we can say that IndusInd Bank and Dena Bank had to bear a loss, meaning they didn't increase their profit but rather decreased it. However, SBI and ICICI Bank didn't fluctuate so much.

5.6.16 Spread or Net Interest Margin (NIM): NIM

being the difference between the interest income and the interest expended as a percentage of total assets shows the ability of the bank to keep the interest on deposits low and interest on advances high. It is an important measure of a bank's core income (income from lending operations). A higher spread indicates the better earnings given the total assets. The *interest income* includes dividend income and *interest expended* includes interest paid on deposits, loan from RBI, and other short term and long term loans (Table 5.16).

Table 5.16: Spread or Net Interest Margin of Selected Banks

Bank	2002-03	2003-04	2004-05	2005-06	Average
ICICI Bank	1.33	1.50	1.69	1.83	1.59
SBI	2.65	2.74	3.03	3.19	2.90
IndusInd Bank	1.80	3.17	4.15	3.15	3.07
Dena Bank	5.68	5.92	6.87	7.23	6.43

Dena Bank gets highest spread and shows its ability to get high interest on deposits and had to pay low on advances. ICICI Bank and SBI improved their position on year-to-year basis. But in the year 2005-06, IndusInd Bank decreased from 4.15 to 3.15.

5.6.17 Net Profit to Average Assets: Profit to average assets indicates the efficiency of the banks in utilizing their assets in generating profits. A higher ratio indicates the better income generating capacity of the assets and better efficiency of management. It is arrived at by dividing the net profit by average assets, which is the average of total assets in the current year and previous year. Thus, this ratio measures the return on assets employed. A higher ratio indicates better earning potential for the future (Table 5.17).

From the Table we can tell that ICICI Bank had better income generating capacity of the assets and better efficiency of management. We cannot tell that IndusInd Bank hadn't had the income generating capacity of the assets but it did not have efficient management, going by the figure which fluctuated, while SBI and Dena Bank tried to improve every year.

Table 5.17: Net Profit to Average Assets (Percent) of Selected Banks

Bank	2002-03	2003-04	2004-05	2005-06	Average
ICICI Bank	1.14	1.41	1.37	1.45	1.34
SBI	0.86	0.94	0.99	1.03	0.96
IndusInd Bank	1.03	0.98	1.05	1.11	1.04
Dena Bank	0.79	0.83	0.95	1.01	0.90

5.6.18 Interest Income to Total Income: Interest income is a basic source of revenue for banks. The interest income to total income indicates the ability of the bank in generating income from its lending. In other words, this ratio measures the income from lending operations as a percentage of the total income generated by the bank in a year. Interest income includes income on advances, interest on deposits with RBI, and dividend income (Table 5.18).

Table 5.18: Interest Income to Total Income (Percent) of Selected Banks

Bank	2002-03	2003-04	2004-05	2005-06	Average
ICICI Bank	74.78	74.37	73.37	75.59	74.53
SBI	84.41	80	82	83.92	82.58
IndusInd Bank	74.24	74.09	81.90	84.01	78.56
Dena Bank	80.22	73.76	84.72	79.32	79.51

SBI gets the highest interest than other banks. In the year of 2004-05, Dena Bank improved from 73.76 to 84.72. All the banks fluctuated but overall income of interest from total income was good. IndusInd Bank did well as it improved every year. It improved from 80 percent to 82 percent in the year 2004-05 and 82 percent to 83.92 percent in the year 2005-

06.

5.6.19 Non-Interest Income to Total Income: Fee-based income accounts for a major portion of the banks' other income. The bank generates higher fee income through innovative products and adapting the technology for sustained service levels. This stream of revenue is not dependent on the bank's capital adequacy and consequent potential to generate income is immense. Thus, this ratio measures the income from operations other than lending as a percentage of total income. Non-interest income is the income earned by the banks excluding income on advances and deposits with RBI. The higher ratio of non-interest income/total income indicates the increasing proportion of fee based income (Table 5.19).

Table 5.19: Non-Interest Income to Total Income (Percent) of Selected Banks

Bank	2002-03	2003-04	2004-05	2005-06	Average
ICICI Bank	25.22	25.63	26.63	25.69	25.79
SBI	15.59	20	18	17.93	17.88
IndusInd Bank	25.76	25.91	18.10	15.99	21.44
Dena Bank	19.78	26.24	15.28	20.68	20.50

From the above data we can tell that ICICI provided innovative products and adapted the technology for sustained service levels. All banks can't maintain the stability and it may be a cause for the competition or any other reason. Here, we can see that IndusInd Bank loosing its level in last two years, it decreased from 18.10 percent to 15.99 percent, while ICICI Bank decreased only by 0.7 percent. In the year 2005-06, Dena Bank improved from 15.28 percent to 20.68 percent, which is because of it providing different innovative services.

5.6.20 Liquid Assets to Total Assets: Liquidity is very important for any organization dealing with money. Banks have to take proper care in hedging liquidity risk while at the same time ensure that a good percentage of funds are invested in higher return generating investments, so that banks can generate profit while at the same time provide liquidity to the depositors. Among assets, cash investments are the most liquid of a bank's assets. The ratios suggested to measure liquidity under CAMEL model are as follows.

Liquid assets include cash in hand, balance with RBI, balance with other banks (both in India and abroad), and money at call and short notice. Total assets include the revaluations of all the assets. The proportion of liquid assets to total assets indicates the overall liquidity position of the bank (Table 5.20).

Table 5.20: Liquid Assets to Total Assets Ratio (Percent) of Selected Banks

Bank	2002-03	2003-04	2004-05	2005-06	Average
ICICI Bank	6.08	6.76	7.71	8.12	7.17
SBI	12.02	10.68	8.55	9.61	10.22
IndusInd Bank	91.24	92.50	91.05	91.93	91.68
Dena Bank	91.20	92.96	94.83	95.33	93.58

Data shows that IndusInd Bank and Dena Bank are capable enough to maintain liquidity. They maintained it at more than 90 percent in the last four years while ICICI Bank and SBI were poor to maintain. But to maintain better liquidity, it affects the profitability of the banks.

5.6.21 Government Securities to Total Assets: Government securities are the most liquid and safe investments. This ratio measures the G-Secs as a proportion of total assets. Banks invests in government securities primarily to meet their SLR requirements which are around 25 percent of net demand and time liabilities. This ratio measures the risk involved in the assets held by a bank (Table 5.21).

From the data we can tell that SBI is the safest bank than others because it invested more than 35 percent in the last 4 years. While ICICI Bank and IndusInd Bank maintained an average, it was not safe. Dena Bank decreased its investment in government securities year by year, which may be profitable, but not safe.

Table 5.21: Government Securities to Total Assets Ratio (Percent) of Selected Banks

Bank	2002-03	2003-04	2004-05	2005-06	Average
ICICI Bank	23.92	23.88	20.57	21.85	22.56
SBI	38.34	38.63	37.39	38.63	38.25
IndusInd Bank	20.40	24.99	21.80	26.01	23.30
Dena Bank	29.65	34.30	33.08	26.49	30.88

5.6.22 Liquid Assets to Demand Deposits: This ratio measures the ability of a bank to meet the demand from deposits in a particular year. It is arrived at by dividing the liquid assets by total demand deposits. Demand deposits offer high liquidity to the depositor and so banks have to invest these assets in a highly liquid form. The liquid assets includes cash in hand, balance with RBI, balance with other banks (both in India and abroad), and money at call and short notice (Table 5.22).

The data shows that the liquidity part for SBI was very low due to the fact that it is in government sector, so the trust is higher than any other private sector bank.

Table 5.22: Liquid Assets to Demand Deposits Ratio (Percent) of Selected Banks

Bank	2002-03	2003-04	2004-05	2005-06	Average
ICICI Bank	175.90	116.70	100.72	103.56	124.22
SBI	100.91	86.63	69.46	71.53	82.13
IndusInd Bank	109.85	162.89	159.20	134.85	141.70
Dena Bank	108.20	106.13	109.04	107.12	107.62

5.6.23 Liquid Assets to Total Deposits: This ratio

measures the liquidity available to the deposits of a bank. Total deposits include demand deposits, saving deposits, term deposits and deposits of other financial institutions. Liquid assets includes cash in hand, balance with RBI, balance with other banks (both in India and abroad), and money at call and short notice (Table 5.23).

Table 5.23: Liquid Assets to Total Deposits Ratio (Percent) of Selected Banks

Bank	2002-03	2003-04	2004-05	2005-06	Average
ICICI Bank	13.47	12.44	12.95	14.19	13.26
SBI	15.26	13.67	10.71	11.56	12.80
IndusInd Bank	10.51	12.46	10.85	10.80	11.15
Dena Bank	11.05	11.23	10.91	10.71	11.06

The above data shows that ICICI Bank gave much better quality of total deposits of a bank. Total deposits include demand deposits, saving deposits, term deposits and deposits of other financial institutions, which shows that even being a private sector bank, the trust is greater than any other bank for ICICI Bank.

References

Bhattacharyya, A., Lovell, C.A.K., and Sahay, P. (1997), "The Impact of Liberalization on the Productive Efficiency of Indian Commercial Banks", European Journal of Operations Research, Vol. 98.

Berger, A.N., Hassan, I., and Zhou, M. (2005), "Ownership, Financial Liberalization, and Efficiency of Chinese Banks," FMA Working Paper Series 2005.

Buch, C.M. (1997), "Opening up for Foreign Banks: How Central and Eastern Europe Can Benefit," Economics of Transition.

Chatterjee, G. (1997), "Scale Economies in Banking: Indian Experience in Deregulated Era", RBI Occasional Papers, Vol. 18, No. 1.

Claessens, S. and Glaessner, T. (1998), "The Internationalization of

Financial Services in Asia," Working Papers - Domestic finance, saving, financial systems, stock markets. 1911, World Bank

Claessens, S., Demirguc-Kunt, A., and Huizinga, H. (2001), "How does foreign entry affect the domestic banking market?" Journal of Banking and Finance, 25.

Das, A., Nag, A., and Ray, S.C. (2004), "Liberalization, Ownership, and Efficiency in Indian Banking: A Nonparametric Approach," Economics Working Papers, University of Connecticut.

Gilbert, R.A. and Wilson, P.W. (1998), "Effects of Deregulation on the Productivity of Korean Banks," Journal of Economics and Business, 50.

Haslem, J. A., Scheraga, C.A. and Bedingfield, J.P. (1999), "DEA efficiency profiles of U.S. banks operating internationally," *International Review of Economics & Finance*, Vol. 8, Issue 2.

Isik, I. and Hassan, M. K. (2003), "Financial Deregulation and Total Factor Productivity Change: An Empirical Study of Turkish Commercial Banks," Journal of Banking & Finance, 27(8).

Websites

www.indsind.com.
www.icicibank.com.
www.ficci.com.
www.hdfcbank.com.
www.onlinesbi.com.
www.economictimes.indiatimes.com.
www.rbi.org.in.
www.business-standard.com.

Bibliography

Bibliography

Al Ebrhar and G. Bennett Stewart III (1999), "The EVA revolution" Journal of Applied Corporate Finance, Vol. 12, No. 2.

Al Ebrhar, Gary Hamel (1997), "Debate: Duking it out over EVA", Fortune, Chicago, p. 232.

Alfred Rappaport (1986), "Creating Shareholder Value, The New Standard for Business performance", The Free Press.

Aswati Damodaran (1998), "Value Creation and Enhancement: Back to the future", Working paper series, Stern School of Business.

Altman, (1968), "Financial ratios discriminate analysis and prediction of corporate Bankruptcy", Journal of Finance, September, 598.

Altman, (2002), "Corporate Distress Prediction models in turbulent Economic and base environment", Journal of Finance, 5.

Abdul Aziz, (1984), "Bankruptcy Prediction and Investigation of cash flow based models", Ph.D. Thesis at Dallas.

Agrawal N.P. and Gupta S.I., "Indian cement industries problems and prospects", Indian journal of Marketing, September 1984.

Beaver, W.H., (1966), "Financial Ratios and predictions of failure empirical research in according selected studies", journal of accounting research, 77-111.

Bacidore, Jeffrey M, Boquist, John A, Milbourn, Todd T, Thakor, Anjan V.(1997), "The search for the best financial performance measure", Financial Analysts Journal Charlottesville, pp. 11-20.

Banerjee, Ashok (1999), "Economic Value Added and shareholder wealth: An Empirical examination", Paradigm, Vol. 3 No.1, pp. 99-133.

Bennett III, Stewart G (1995), "EVA works: but not if you make these common mistakes", Fortune, Chicago, pp.

117-118.

Biddle, Bowen and Wallace, (1999), "Evidence on EVA", Journal of Applied Corporate Finance, Volume 12, No. 2.

Barnes, A. James. (1964), "A Pedagogic Note on Cost of Capital," Journal of Finance, March, pp. 65-85.

Baumol, William and Durton G. Michael (1967), "The Firm's Optimal Debt-Equity Combination and the Cost of Capital", Quarterly Journal of Economics, November, pp. 60-75.

Bhat Ramesh, (1980), "Determinants of Financial Leverage: Some Further Evidence", The Chartered Accountant, December, pp. 451-456.

Bhayani S.J., (2006), "Financial Leverage and Its Impact on Shareholders' Return: A Study of Indian Cement Industry", International Journal of Management Science, Vol. 2, No. 1, July, pp. 31-42.

Bacidore, Jeffrey M, Boquist, John A, Milbourn, Todd T, Thakor, Anjan V.(1997), "The search for the best financial performance measure", Financial Analysts Journal Charlottesville, pp. 11-20.

Blinder A. S. and L. J. Maccini (1991), "The Resurgence of Inventory Research: What Have We Learned?", Journal of Economic Survey, Vol. 5, pp. 291-328.

Bhayani, S.J. (2004), Practical Financial Statements, Raj Book Enterprise, Jaipur.

Bhayani S. J. (2004), "Working Capital and Profitability Relationship (A Case Study of Gujarat Ambuja Cements Ltd.)", SCMS Indian Management, April-June, pp. 98-111.

Bose Indramil and Agarwal anurag, (2001), "Prediction of Survival and attrition of click and mortar Corporations" Reports submitted to Department of decision and information sciences, Warrington College of Business University of Florida, Gainesville.

Bhalla, V.K. (2002), Financial Management and Policy, Anmol Publication, New Delhi.

Bhalla, V.K (2001-02), Financial Management and Policy. Anmol Publication, New Delhi.

Chakraborty P.K. (2005), "Working Capital Management: A Case Study of Cadila Health Care Ltd.", ICFAI Reader, Hyderabad, May, pp. 57-63.

Chatterjee, M (2007), "Global Scenario of Steel and Perspective", Steel Scenario Journal, Kolkata, Vol. 16/Q3, p. editorial address.

Chatterjee, M (2007), "World Steel Industry and India", Steel Scenario Journal, Kolkata, Vol. 16/Q4, p. editorial address.

Clay, M. J. and Walley, B. H. (1965), Performance and Profitability, Longmans, London, p. 184.

Chandrasekhar, (1997), "Financial Leverage: Its Determinants and its Impact on Cost of Capital and Shareholders' Return, Journal of Accounting and Finance, Vol. XI, No. 2, pp. 82-93.

Durand, David (1960), "The use of Debt and Equity Fund in Business: Trends and problems of measurement", in Ezra Solomon (Ed) The Management of Corporate Capital. New York. The Free Press of Glencoe, pp. 230-245.

Dutta S. K., "Investment: A Test of Alternative Concepts," Journal of Finance, September, pp. 110-25.

Eidleman Gregous, (1995), "Z scores guidance to failure prediction", CPA journal online", February 4.

Fraenkel, J.R. and Wallen, N.E. (1990), How to design and evaluate research in education, McGraw-Hill, New York.

Gupta, L.C. (1999), "Financial ratio as forewarning indicators of corporative sickness", Bombay ICICI, XIX (4)37.

Gupta, R.L. and Radhasway M., (1995), Financial management analysis, 5th edition, Sultan Chand & Sons, New Delhi, 45.

Gangudhar V. (1998), "Financial analysts of companies in Erita: A profitability and Efficiency Focus" The management accountant, Volume 33, No. 11/ November.

Gentry, E. J. (1976), Faculty Working Paper, College of

Commerce and Business Administration, University of Illinois, 1976.

Hyderabad, R.L. (1995), "Management of Liquidity and profitability", Vol. XI.

Hatem Ben Amecs, (2003), "Assessing Bankrupt Probabilities of American Firms", A Logistic Approach, pp. 115-120.

Herbron, (2003), "Institute of Professional Accountant graduate of business and Multi-dimensional graphics and banks prediction", Journal of Accounting Research, 21(1), pp. 297-299.

Hiram, S. Davis (1955), Productivity Accounting, op. cit. p.13

Haley, Charles W. (1966), "A note on the Cost of Debt: Journal of Financial and Statistical Analysis, December, pp. 160-80.

Khan & Jain, (1997), Financial Management, 5th edition, Tata McGraw Hill Publishing Company Ltd, 45.

Krishna Chaitanya V, (2005), "Measuring financial distress of IDBI using Altman Z scores Model", The ICFAI Journal of Bank Management, pp. 6-15.

Kulkarni, P.V. and Sathyaprasad B.G., (2000), Financial management, 9th edition, Himalaya Publishing Company, 35.

Kiang Melody Y. et al, (2005), "Understand corporate rationales for Engaging in Reverse in stock splits –A data Mining Application" Proceeding of 38th Hawaii International conference on system sciences, California state University, long beach, pp. 7-15.

Kar A. P., "Need for cost and Management control in Indian Tea Industry", the management accountant; Calcutta December 1995.

Kothari C.R. (2004), Research Methodology Methods and Techniques, New Age International publishers, New Delhi. pp. 256-264.

Khan and Jain, (1987), Management Accounting, Tata McGraw Hill, New Delhi.

Langemaler, R. M., (2004), "Financial Ratios used in Financial management", Financial Management, Kansos State University October, 40.

Malik A. K. and Sur D, (1998), "Working Capital and Profitability: A Case Study in interrelation". The Management Accountant, Kolkata, November, pp. 805-809.

Malik A.K. and Sur D. (1999), "Working Capital and Profitability: A Case Study of Hindustan Lever Ltd." Finance India, Delhi, September, pp. 857-871.

Pandey I.M. (1991), Financial Management, Vikas Publishing House, New Delhi.

Pandey I.M., (1985), "The Financial Leverage in India: A Study", Indian Management, March.

Rej, D. and Sur, D. (2001), "Profitability analysis of Indian food products industry", Vol. xi.

Rose T. (1975), The Internal Finance of Industrial Undertaking, London: Pitman and Sons Ltd., pp. 221-32.

Roy, C.D. (1972), "The Concept of Cost of Capital", The Management Accountant India, September, pp. 554-55

Sarma L. & Rao K., (1969), "Leverage and Value of the Firm", Journal of Finance, Sept., pp. 25-30.

Solomon Ezra (1963), "Leverage and the Cost of Capital; Journal of Finance, May, pp. 330-65.

Scott, J.J. (1997), "Bankruptcy, Secured Debt and Optimal Capital Structure", Journal of Finance, March, pp. 60-72.

Schall, Lawrence D. and Charles W. Harley (1977), Introduction to Financial Management, 2nd Ed. New York: McGraw-Hill Book Company, p. 801.

Sharma, N.K. (1988), Prateeksha Publications, Jaipur.

Venkatesan S. (1983), "Determinants of Financial Leverage an Empirical Extension", The Chartered Accountant, January, pp. 519-527.

Van Horne James C, (2002), "Financial Management Policy", 12th edition, Pearson Education Asia, 67.

Van Horne James and Wachowicz john M., (2005), "Fundamental of financial management", 11th edition,

Prentice Hall of India Pvt. Ltd, New Delhi, pp. 125-167.

Index

Index